CW00743069

"Asleep in the Deep"

The Story of the Rise and Fall of the

Bennett Steamship Company

Diane Brian

rainbow
publishing

ISBN 978 0 9571169 0 0

Cover design by York Publishing Services Ltd.

Prepared and printed by:
York Publishing Services Ltd.
Tel: 01904 431213 Website: www.yps-publishing.co.uk

This book is dedicated to my mother

CONTENTS

Foreword

I first encountered the name Bennett when I found out that my mother shares the same name as her grandmother Mary Adelaide Bennett. My mother often told me that the Bennett line of the family was quite wealthy but more than that I didn't know. My grandmother had in her possession a company report and balance sheet for the Bennett Steamship Company dated 1930. It was later that I discovered my grandfather was a shareholder in this company. From these few sketchy details, I embarked on my research. As the facts emerged, the story became more and more interesting, and I decided that I should attempt to publish it. The company was started by my great-great-grandfather John Bennett. In writing the story, I wanted to place events in John's family life into context by setting them against the social background of his home town of Goole. At the same time, I thought it would be useful to interweave these family events with historical events, both local and national, that were taking place during this time. John involved himself in numerous business ventures ultimately leading to the establishment and subsequent success of his company. In a cruel twist of fate world events finally bring about the eventual downfall of his shipping 'empire'. I hope that my account remains true to the facts and will bring alive the history of this company and the life of its founder John Bennett.

Chapter 1
In the Beginning

In order to begin this story it is only fair to start by telling a little of the couple responsible for bringing John Bennett into this world, his parents Thomas and Hannah.

Hannah Mason, John's mother, baptised 26th August 1805 at Whitgift Parish Church, is the daughter of John Mason and his wife Mary nee Bentley. Educated at Reedness School, Hannah later takes up a position as domestic help at a farm house in Adlingfleet.

Thomas Bennett, John's father, baptised 1st January 1797 is the son of farmer Thomas Bennett and his wife Ann nee Cooke. In Baines Trade Directory of 1822, Thomas Bennett appears as Parish Clerk for Adlingfleet. Thomas from Adlingfleet, meets Hannah Mason from Whitgift, and they marry on the 12th November 1826 at St Mary Magdalene Parish Church, Whitgift.

More detailed information about Thomas and Hannah is given by Susannah Everatt whilst recounting her family history. A transcript of Susannah's original notes, deposited at Goole Local Studies Library, is for the benefit of family history research.

The newly married couple live close to the old river Don where it flows towards the river Trent. In this home Thomas and Hannah have their first son, whom they baptise John, on the 27th July 1827. He lives for only a few months, and they bury him 21st January 1828 at All Saints Church, Adlingfleet.

Hannah gives birth to their first daughter Ann on 1st April 1829 and they baptise her on the 25th April.

A Mr. Empson of Ousefleet Hall proposes to the Bennetts that they should take Sandhill Farm near the small hamlet of Eastoft in the East Riding of Yorkshire. The Bennetts accept and settle themselves into their new home. It is here that their second son John is born on the 17th March 1836 and baptised on the 10th April. John, the subject of this story, is seven years younger than his sister Ann. Four years later along comes another son, baptised Thomas (after his father) on the 2nd September 1840. Sadly he dies after just two days. Three years later Hannah gives birth to their second daughter, baptised Mary, on the 27th June 1843. Mary lives for only three weeks and they bury her on 17th July 1843. The family baptise all of their children at All Saints Parish Church, Adlingfleet. Thomas and Hannah have just two surviving children, Ann and John.

Thomas and Hannah Bennett can be seen in the census for 1841 transcribed in *figure 1*. The farm is within the parish of Adlingfleet and Thomas Bennett's occupation is given as farmer. The family employs one female 'farm servant' Mary Manuel, aged 25. At this time, the census shows servants employed in the domestic sphere as 'House Servant'. Later census forms include more detailed categories of service such as dairy maid and scullery maid. It can only be assumed that she helped out generally on the farm, but the exact role she played is open to speculation. Also living in this household is Wilson Bentley age 45 and an 'Independent'. This is quite a statement for those times. He can be seen again in the 1851 census, living with his brother John and sister-in-law Ann - see *figure 5*. Wilson is uncle to Hannah Bennett. In later research, Wilson and Hannah are found, with matching headstones, buried in adjoining graves in the family plot at Whitgift Church. According to Wilson's headstone he dies at the age of 97.

Figure 1 – Census 1841 – Adlingfleet

Place	Houses		Names	Age		Profession, Trade, Employment or of Independent Means	Where Born	
	Un	Inh		Male	Female		Whether Born in same county	Whether Born in Scotland, Ireland or Foreign Parts
Adlingfleet		1	Thomas Bennett	40		Farmer	Y	
			Hannah Bennett		35		Y	
			Ann Bennett		12		Y	
			John Bennett	5			Y	
			Wilson Bentley	45		Independent	Y	
			Mary Manuel		25	Farm Servant	Y	

Un=Uninhabited house   Inh=Inhabited house

3

In the 1881 census, two years before his death, his age is also curiously 97 and he is in the household of Hannah Bennett as a 'boarder' with an occupation of 'landed proprietor'. In 1841 the young John is 5 years of age, his sister Ann 12.

Thomas Bennett owns land in villages around Goole. This provides him with valuable extra income since some of it is in the occupation of tenants. In a sale dated 21st September 1841, Thomas sells one small croft measuring 1 acre 3 roods and 20 perches "with premises recently occupied by George Osbaldeston Esquire". The buyer, Thomas Turner Pearson, pays the grand sum of £200.[1]

Five years later on 8th October 1846, Ann age 17, marries John Brunyee of Elm Tree House, Eastoft. Ann's brother John is only 10 years of age when his big sister leaves the family home.

At this time facts are thin on the ground, and the 10-yearly census provides a glimpse into the Bennett household. *Figure 4* shows the 1851 census return for Thomas and Hannah Bennett. Although Thomas Bennett's farm is not vast, it is big enough to warrant employing two labourers. One of these is George Stark who is living with the family. The other labourer did not reside in the household. In addition, the family employs a House Servant, Mary Welch, from Ireland. It is not clear however if the two labourers included, or excluded, the two named servants. Also seen at this time is that Thomas Bennett's grandson, Thomas John Brunyee aged 3, is in the household. He is born 5th May 1847 and baptised May 30th, the first child of their daughter Ann (now Brunyee). Ann has just had her third child, George, born before the 1851 census, which may explain why Thomas John is with his grandparents. Ann and her husband John go on to have a total of fourteen children.

Figure 2
Hannah Bennett,
baptised 26th
August 1803,
buried 7th
September 1883

Figure 3
Ann Bennett,
baptised 25th
April 1829
died 28th June
1900

Figure 4 – Census 1851 –Adlingfleet

Person	Relationship To Head Of Family	Cond*	Age		Rank, Profession Or Occupation	Where Born
			Male	Female		
Thomas Bennett	Head	Mar	54		Farmer of 86 acres +	Yorks, Adlingfleet
Hannah Bennett	Wife	Mar		45	Farmer's wife	Yorks, Reedness
John Bennett	Son	U	15		Farmer's son	Yorks, Adlingfleet
Thomas John Brunyee	Grandson		3			Yorks, Adlingfleet
George Stark	Servant	U	28		Farmer's labourer	Lincs, Thealby
Mary Welch	Servant	U		16	House Servant	Ir[e]land

+ ..employing 2 labourers Adlingfleet Common

*Condition   Mar=married   U=unmarried

6

Figure 5 – Census 1851 – Reedness

Person	Relationship To Head Of Family	Cond*	Age		Rank, Profession Or Occupation	Where Born
			Male	Female		
John Bentley	Head	Mar	55		Landed Proprietor	Yorks, Reedness
Ann Bentley	Wife	Mar		52		Yorks, Selby
Wilson Bentley	Brother	U	62		Landed Proprietor	Yorks, Reedness

*Condition   Mar = married   U = unmarried

7

Now aged 15, John Bennett is very much involved with his parents' farm. Such experience would allow him to learn the 'tricks of the trade' and put this into practice later in life. John is soon to become a successful farmer and merchant, and as he nears maturity is about to meet a young lady later to become his wife.

The young lady in question is Sarah Ann daughter of John and Charlotte Sykes (nee Ward) born 14th January 1842, baptised on the 31st January. John and Charlotte Sykes have only two children, Sarah Ann, being their first child, and four years later a son, Robert, born in 1846. This is very similar to the Bennett children, Ann and John, who have seven years separating their births. John Sykes like Thomas Bennett, is also a farmer, and it is easy to speculate that a union between Bennett and Sykes may have been on the cards from early beginnings. Sarah's brother Robert Sykes goes on to raise his eleven children (one of his daughters - Hannah Mary - being my maternal great grandmother) and also farms at Sand Hill, Adlingfleet. There is a close link between the families of Sykes and Bennett, and this will be seen throughout this story.

Chapter 2
Early Married Life

Two events happen within the space of six weeks in 1859. On the 17th May John Bennett marries Sarah Ann Sykes at her birthplace, Crowle. The marriage certificate records, John aged 23, bachelor, with the occupation of farmer. Sarah Ann aged 18 recorded as a spinster. She was, in fact, 17, and some years younger than her husband. They were both able to sign their names despite a claim that John could not read or write, and their witnesses were John Sykes (presumably Sarah Ann's father), Joseph Pindar, and Ann Eliza Linton.

It is then just less than six weeks later that John's father Thomas Bennett dies at the age of 62, buried on the 27th June 1859 at All Saints Church, Adlingfleet. Possibly he had already fallen ill, and handed some of the farm over to his son John, shown as a farmer in the 1861 census. In Thomas Bennett's will proven at Wakefield 3rd August 1859, he leaves effects valued at under £300.[2] On the 13th July 1859, John Bennett is buying back the land his father sold to Thomas Turner Pearson in 1841.[3]

John and Sarah Ann start their family on the 7th August 1860, when their first child, a son, is born at Sand Hill, Adlingfleet. Baptised Thomas (after his grandfather) on the 28th August, the register gives his parents as John and 'Mary Ann'. The minister makes a note beside this event stating 'private'. Such baptisms were often the case with sick children. They bury their son, less than a week later, on the 3rd September at All Saints Church, Adlingfleet. The birth certificate states Thomas's mother as Sarah Ann, so it looks as if the minister made a slight mistake with her name on the baptism entry.

By 1861, John, married for two years, is the head of an already medium sized household, and has the occupation of farmer of 40 acres. The census account can be seen in *figure 6*. Living with the newly married couple is John's widowed mother Hannah Bennett, aged 56. Also with the family is Thomas John Brunyee, John's nephew, who is also present in 1851. Whether he lived with them continually, throughout this 10-year period is not known. He may have come back to help out at the comparatively young age of only 13 with the occupation of 'carter'. John also has two servants – Hannah Cave aged 21 and a Dairy Maid born at Reedness, and Daniel Cook aged 19 a Carter, born in Derrythorpe, Lincolnshire. Both single, as was usually the case with those in service. Normally upon marriage they would leave this profession. Later that year sees the birth of John and Sarah Ann's second son, baptised John after his father, on 29th December 1861, at St Bartholomew's Church, Eastoft. This is also the Church used by Ann Brunyee, John's sister, to baptise her children. John would be educated at a private school and goes on to play a pivotal role in his father's business some years later.

Another land sale in 1862 names John Bennett in the transaction. This indenture dated 25th October 1862 is for five parcels of land in Reedness.[4] Parties named are Thomas Thompson (of Ferrybridge, Farmer); Mary Thompson (of Reedness, Widow); John Howard (of Knottingley, Rope Manufacturer); John Bentley (late of Reedness now of Ferrybridge, Farmer); John Bennett (of Adlingfleet, Farmer); Samuel Rhodes (of Knottingley, Ship-owner). Some of the parcels of land, stated as formerly in the hands of the late George Thompson, suggest that his widow, Mary Thompson, may be selling them, but it is difficult to determine who is buying and who is selling what exactly.

Figure 6 – Census 1861 – Adlingfleet

Abode	Person	Relationship To Head Of Family	Cond*	Age		Rank, Profession Or Occupation	Where Born
				Male	Female		
Sandhill Farm	John Bennett	Head	Mar	25		Farmer of 40 acres	Yorks, Adlingfleet
	Sarah A Bennett	Wife	Mar		20	Farmer's wife	Lincs, Crowle
	Hannah Bennett	Mother	W		56		Yorks, Reedness
	Thomas J Brunyee	Nephew		13		Carter	Yorks, Adlingfleet
	Hannah Cave	Servant	Un		21	Dairy Maid	Yorks, Reedness
	Daniel Cook	Servant	Un	19		Carter	Lincs, Derrythorpe

*Condition   Mar=married   U=unmarried   W=Widow

11

Two and a half years later, along comes another son, Herbert Thomas, baptised 22nd May 1864. Herbert Thomas would go on to be a prominent figure of society in his own right, becoming a J.P. and a key player in his father's business empire. The following year another son, Robert, is born and baptised 9th April 1865. Like his two brothers before him, Robert's father would place him in a key position of responsibility in the family business which involved his leaving England for France.

On the 22nd March 1866, John Bennett signs an agreement with Basil T Wood Esquire MP of Conyngham Hall Knaresborough to rent Sandhill Farm (near Adlingfleet).[5] This is for a term of 21 years beginning from 5th April 1866 with an annual rent of £250. John Bennett is responsible for insuring to the sum of at least £800, and with a company approved by the owner. The farm comprises 130 acres 3 roods and 22 perches. It is unclear on what basis he occupied Sandhill Farm prior to this.

On the 25th August 1866, the first of the daughters comes along, with the arrival of Annie Charlotte baptised on the 28th October. This story goes on to tell of her relatively short life. A second daughter, my great grandmother Mary Adelaide, arrives three years later. She is affectionately known within the family circle as 'Pollie'. Mary Adelaide, baptised 13th June 1869, takes her name from the fashion of the time in naming girls after Queen Adelaide. My mother is named after her.

At this juncture, a certain distraction comes over John Bennett. Her name is Mary Ann Sykes. Mary Ann is born in Luddington, a small hamlet in Yorkshire, not many miles away from John Bennett's birthplace of Adlingfleet. Baptised 22nd December 1844, Mary Ann is the daughter of George Sykes (born Fockerby and later farmer at Brind, near Howden) and his wife Elizabeth (nee Everatt) born Eastoft. Mary Ann is eight years younger than John. It is highly likely that, with the extremely strong links between the Bennetts and the Sykes, John would have known of, and most likely have met, the younger Mary Ann Sykes at some time during their lives up to this point. Mary Ann Sykes marries her cousin Richard Robinson Sykes on 26th March 1867 at Howden, and they apparently live at Brind House at the beginning of their marriage. Both their fathers at this time are farmers. Richard Robinson Sykes baptised 5th August 1842, is the son of Richard Sykes of Fockerby (brother of Mary Ann's father George) and Mary Robinson, of Amcotts. Richard and Mary Sykes lived at Whins Gate Farm, Fockerby. There are some accounts that Richard Robinson and Mary Ann's first child is a son George; there is no trace of this child. Tragedy strikes on the 1st September 1869, when Richard dies at Adlingfleet. His death certificate gives his age as 27 years, and his occupation as farmer. The cause of death given on the certificate is, "congestion of the brain 3 weeks bronchitis 2 days certified". The informant present at his death is Ann Armitage of Swinefleet, and she signs her name with a cross. After his death, registered 2nd Sept 1869 by registrar John Wilmot, Richard is buried in All Saints Church, Adlingfleet on the 4th September. John Bennett helps Mary Ann to manage the family estate after the death of her young husband leaves her distraught with grief. According to family sources John falls in love with the beautiful Mary Ann Sykes – the young widow. The following year Mary Ann gives birth to a son, John Henry. Baptised on 3rd April 1870 at St Bartholomew's Church, Eastoft, the vicar T W Sewell lists the parents as Richard and Mary Ann Sykes, and also writes beside the baptism that "Richard Sykes dies before this child is born".

In 1870, John Bennett enters into an agreement with two other men to purchase and take over the title to a freehold estate in the parish of Snaith. John, named as a merchant, joins together with Benjamin Shaw of Goole farmer, and Henry Shaw of Cowick, to take over the freehold title to the Cowick Hall Estate left in trust to Viscount Hugh Richard Downe.[6] On the 9th December 1869, Viscount Downe sells for £80,000 exclusive of timber valued at £8004:1:0; the total purchase price being £88004:1:0. In the same transaction the purchasers then sell the following parts of the estate to:

Thomas Harsley Carnochan for £7964:13:0 (inclusive of timber); Thomas and Robert England (Tenants in Common) for £30,474 (inclusive of timber); John Humble Rockett for £8993:3:0 (inclusive of timber); John, Jane and Mary Corner (Tenants in Common) for £5693:13:0 (inclusive of timber); and Shepherd Freeman for £11,152:1:0 (inclusive of timber).

John, Benjamin, and Henry are then left to pay £23,726:11:0 for the remaining parts of the estate.

Later in the same year, John's wife Sarah Ann gives birth to her seventh child, a daughter – named after her – Sarah Ann. Sarah Ann's baptism on 8th December 1870 has the note 'private' written against it. Maybe Sarah Ann believed this would be her last child since it appears relatively late in line to pass on her name.

John now has two ladies in his life, and this can be seen through the window of the census of 1871 – firstly looking at John Bennett's family installed at Sandhill Farm - see *figure 7*. Two of John and Sarah Ann's children are absent from the household – their eldest son John, and their eldest daughter – Annie Charlotte. John can be found at a private school in Goole run by Edward Cragg Haynes BA and Clergyman - see *figure 8*. Also at the school are two Brunyee children – Frederick age 13, and John Henry age 11 – the fourth and fifth sons of Ann Brunyee (nee Bennett) and the young John Bennett's cousins. They are also sharing their classroom with a young man from Abo in Finland. The Bennett family are now employing three servants, perhaps due to the increasing household. John's nephew Thomas John Brunyee is no longer shown in the household (or certainly not on the night of the census). There are two domestic servants – Ann Hunt, aged 20 born Amcotts, Lincolnshire, and Sarah Bennett, at the

14

Figure 7 – Census 1871 – Adlingfleet

Abode	Person	Relationship To Head Of Family	Cond*	Age		Rank, Profession Or Occupation	Where Born
				Male	Female		
Sandhill Farm	John Bennett	Head	Mar	35		Merchant & Farmer	Yorks, Adlingfleet
	Sarah A Bennett	Wife	Mar		29	Farmer's wife	Lincs, Crowle
	Herbert Thomas Bennett	Son		7			Yorks, Adlingfleet
	Robert Bennett	Son		6			Yorks, Adlingfleet
	Mary Adelaide Bennett	Dau			2		Yorks, Adlingfleet
	Sarah Ann Bennett	Dau			1		Yorks, Adlingfleet
	Ann Hunt	Servant	Unm		20	Domestic Servant	Lincs, Amcotts
	Sarah Bennett	Servant	Unm		15	Domestic Servant	Yorks, Siston
	Thomas Spriggs	Servant	Unm	29		Servant	Lincs, Crowle

*Condition   Mar = Married   Unm = Unmarried

age of 15 born Siston, Yorkshire. It is unclear whether this Sarah Bennett could be related to the family. The family also employs a male servant, Thomas Spriggs, aged 29 born in Crowle, Lincolnshire.

This census shows that John Bennett is no longer employed solely as a farmer, but as a merchant and farmer. Also that John's mother Hannah Bennett no longer lives with her married son. Perhaps the increasing family resulted in lack of space, or maybe a touch of the 'mother-in-law blues'. Hannah is to be found as head of her own household with her uncle Wilson Bentley living with her – see *figure 9*. They are both described as annuitants. They have two farm servants and one domestic servant. Her uncle John Bentley had died by this time, and his widow Ann found in a separate household, with a general domestic servant of 70 years of age! Hannah's age given on this census does not quite fit with her apparent year of birth – 1805.

Where is Mary Ann Sykes to be found? She lives at 34 Cartwright Street in Doncaster with her infant son John Henry – see *figure 11*. Cartwright Street no longer exists, now lost beneath the Waterdale Shopping Centre and car park. Her occupation of 'Retired Farmer' suggests that she is self supported financially by her late husband's estate, and as may also be supposed, by the wealthy John Bennett. As a merchant and prominent farmer, it would be reasonably likely that John Bennett would be in contact with the Doncaster area, as this was a principle market town at the time. He is later connected with the building of Goole and Doncaster Market Halls. There is no evidence of Mary Ann's first child – George - to her late husband. Perhaps just the name was incorrect from the family story, and he is, in fact, the John Henry in the census document.

Figure 8 - Census 1871- Goole (following image)

16

Abode	Person	Relationship To Head	Cond*	Age Male	Age Female	Rank, Prof. Or Occ.	Where Born
Empson Villa (Private school)	Edward Cragg Haynes	Head	Mar	49		Clergyman +	WI#, Barbados
	Henrietta Haynes	Wife	Mar		48		Lincs,Gainsboro
	Edmond Fowler Haynes	Son		7			Yorks, Swinefleet
	Waldemar Canute Granberg	Boarder		16			Finland, Abo
	Walter William Strickland	Boarder		13			Yorks, Carlton
	Frederick Brunyee	Boarder		13			Lincs, Eastoft
	John Rank	Boarder		13			Yorks, Hull
	John Dunn Thornton	Boarder		13			Yorks, Swinefleet
	George Dunn Thornton	Boarder		11			Yorks, Swinefleet
	John Henry Brunyee	Boarder		11			Swinefleet
	Thomas Hugh Miller	Boarder		9			Bedford, Woburn
	John Bennett	Boarder		9			Yorks, Adlingfleet
	William Henry Frank Miller	Boarder		7			Bedford, Woburn
	Mary Jane Lilford	Servant	UnM		21		Yorks, Thorne

*Condition   Mar=Married   UnM=Unmarried   + BA Cambridge   #WI = West Indies

Figure 9 – Census 1871 – Reedness

Abode	Person	Relationship To Head Of Family	Cond*	Age		Rank, Profession Or Occupation	Where Born
				Male	Female		
	Hannah Bennett	Head	W		58	Annuitant	Yorks, Reedness
	Wilson Bentley	Uncle	Unm	73		Annuitant	Yorks, Reedness
	Jonah Holmes	Serv	Mar	47		Farm Servant	Yorks, Hook
	Hannah Holmes	Serv	Mar		47	Domestic Servant	Yorks, Laxton
	John Sheppard	Serv	Unm	16		Farm Servant	Sunderland

*Condition   W=Widow   Mar=Married   UnM=Unmarried

18

One can imagine the business trips and diversions John must have manufactured to spend time with his beloved Mary Ann. Nine months later Mary Ann loses her son at the age of only 21 months. This must have been a truly sad time for her, and she must have felt utterly alone.

Figure 10 is a photograph taken of High Street Doncaster in 1875. This would have been the town as Mary Ann knew it at this time, and a street she must have walked along almost daily as she lived close to the centre of town.

Figure 10 High Street from Hall Gate, Doncaster, 1875

Figure 11 - Census 1871 – Doncaster

Abode	Person	Relationship To Head Of Family	Cond*	Age		Rank, Profession Or Occupation	Where Born
				Male	Female		
34 Cartwright Street	Mary Ann Sykes	Head	Widow		26	Retired Farmer	Luddington, Lincs
	John H Sykes	Son		1			Yorks, Fockerby

*Condition

Chapter 3
The Start of the Family Empire

A history of the Bennett Steamship Company, written in 1947 by Albert Chatelle[7], describes the business of John Bennett around 1870 as follows.

"Shortly after the war of 1870 an important English Importer of merchandise imported each season into Hull and Goole important cargoes of fruit, vegetables and above all – potatoes that had been shipped in one of the Channel Ports"

Business must have prospered, for in 1872 John Bennett purchases Grove House in Old Goole, which had belonged to his father's friend. Mr and Mrs Empson owners of Goole Hall and Empson Hall had previously lived there, and had now moved to Bleak House Corner, a double fronted house, close to the river Don, in Old Goole. A Mr Stones, around this time, purchases Mount Pleasant, selling it later to Major Brothers. Mount Pleasant would also become the property of John Bennett in the not too distant future.

At the time of the 1871 census, Grove House is occupied by David Briggs (born Selby, Yorkshire) aged 70, a 'Grazier Occupier' of 59 acres and his much younger wife, Emma L Briggs (born Harewood, Yorkshire) aged 46. With them are their two servants – Anne Johnson, aged 24 (born Thorne, Yorkshire) and William Haigh, aged 20 (born Goole, Yorkshire). Perhaps they were eager to move to a smaller place in light of Mr Briggs' years. *Figure 12* is a map of Old Goole from 20 years later. This map shows the position of

21

Grove House on Swinefleet Road, with 'Bennett's Jetty' at the bottom of the garden.

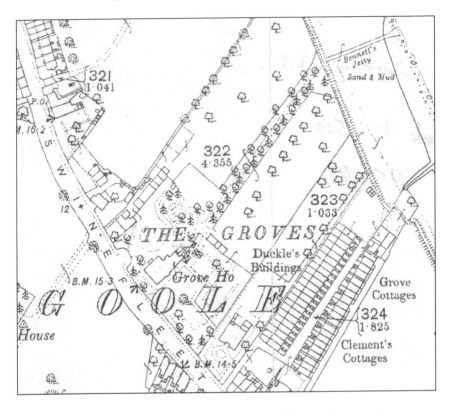

Figure 12 – map of Old Goole from Ordnance Survey 1892

On 4th April 1872, an Indenture registers the transfer of deed for Grove House from Robert Cornelius Empson and Elizabeth Cornwell Empson to John Bennett.[8] This property consisted of two messuages or tenements with gardens and barns, stables and outbuildings, and portions of land behind them in the township of Goole amounting to 3 acres, 1 rood, and 28 perches. The northern boundary is the river Ouse. To the south is the highway from Goole to Swinefleet. Land to the east belongs to Robert Empson who is in the process of selling this to John Bennett. The western side comprises premises belonging to Mr William Hardisly Clark, lately occupied by David Briggs and George Greenfield. At the time of this deed, the premises to the west are owned jointly by David Briggs and John Bennett. On the same day another deed is registered.[9] Robert Cornelius Empson of Ousefleet and his wife Elizabeth Cornwell Empson transfer the deed of property consisting of a messuage or farmhouse with barn, stables, other outbuildings and yard or garth adjoining at Swinefleet including pieces of arable and grassland in Reedness and Swinefleet. This totalled 133 acres 2 roods and 9 perches and had been in the occupation of Samuel Smith, probably a tenant. This property can be identified as Key Field Farm due to the matching of field names such as 'Upper Sands', 'Long Shores', 'Puddiners' etc with an itinerary of property valued for John Bennett in 1885 (covered in more detail later). The deed includes a schedule of the individual fields included.

Two years later on the 17th April 1874, John Bennett (then described as merchant) sells 361 square yards of land in The Groves to the Reverend Edward Cragg Haynes of Goole, Clerk.[10] Rev. Haynes is the proprietor of the private school, Empson Villa, attended by John Bennett junior. This land adjoins another property already owned by Edward Cragg Haynes. On the same day, another significant acquisition of property takes place when John Bennett purchases New Fields from The Right Honourable Thomas Henry Sutton Sotheron-Estcourt of Estcourt, Gloucestershire.[11] This area, in the town of Goole, lies between North Street and Ellen's View, and consists of 16 acres and 12 perches. It has a boundary to the north made up of land owned by William Clarke Esquire. North Street forms the southern boundary. The western boundary is land belonging to Mrs English, Mr James Rex, and the North Eastern Railway Company. On the east bound by land belonging to Richard Duckles, Richard Freeman, the late Thomas Bromley and the highway from Goole to Hook. From 1874, Edinburgh, Alexandra, Carlisle and other streets and terraces are laid out. Burlington Crescent is a handsome curved main street of principal properties and divides the area down the middle. In October of the following year, John Bennett advertises this land for sale as building plots. The plan shows the area as individual lots (see close-up section) and numbered accordingly (*figure 13*).[12] A later Ordnance Survey map of 1905 (*figure 14*) shows the area (outlined) with the streets fully developed.

The splendid photograph in *figure 15* is Grove House at a period somewhat later than this point in the story. The house has some significant extensions and modification work carried out when the two families combine after the death of Sarah Ann Bennett in 1888. The house is extended around 1889 by the addition of a 'wing' to the right of the large bay window that carefully copies the original style. A similar close-up photograph shows a plaque above the window in the extension bearing this date together with John Bennetts' initials. This grand house clearly demonstrates the enormous wealth John Bennett enjoys for his strenuous efforts in business. The figures in the garden are quite likely family members but cannot be positively identified.

At this point in the story, John Bennett and Mary Ann Sykes have their son, Arthur Frederick (registered Sykes) born at Doncaster in 1871.[13] He would go on to become a marine engineer following in his father's line of work in the shipping industry. John's wife Sarah Ann does not have another (and her last) child for three more years. It is to be two years to the arrival of the third of John and Mary Ann's children – Isabel – on the 13th September 1873 born at 'East Beach' Lytham and registered with her mother's surname - Sykes.[14] By this time, for some reason, Mary Ann is choosing to give birth to her children on the opposite side of the country, in Lancashire. It is said that she had relations there, and perhaps the support she needed at these times, was more than John could give her, what with his active business life, and his other family. Although the precise address is not known, the 1881 census reveals that East Beach was a fairly respectable neighbourhood, with most residents being private, and well-to-

Figure 13 Plan of Bennett's Town Goole May 1874

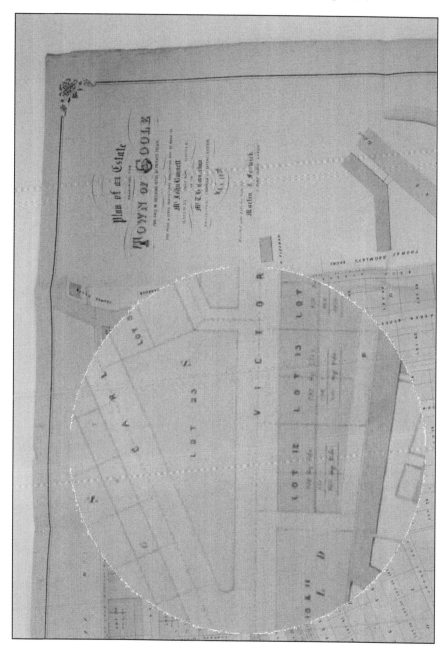

Figure 14 Map of Old Goole from Ordnance Survey 1905

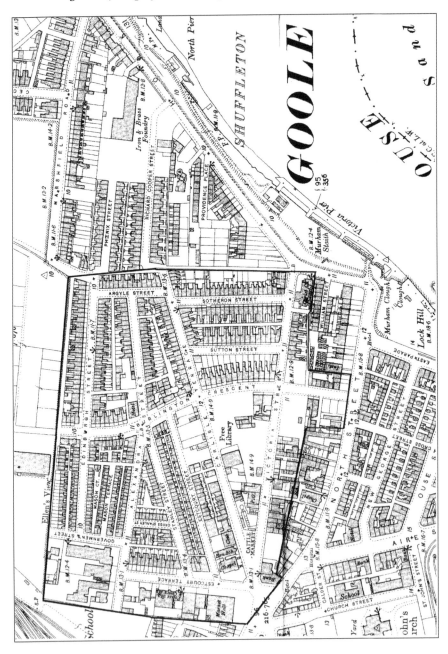

Figure 15 – Grove House (some time post 1889)

do individuals, such as merchants, business men, retirees & annuitants. There are also a large number of 'Lodging House Keepers'. It cannot be determined whether Mary Ann gives birth at a private address or in a lodging house. It must have been quite an ordeal in the Victorian age for her to go through this experience, and then register her daughter on the 26th September without naming the father. In 1874, it was Sarah Ann's turn again, when along comes their eighth and last child – Albert Edmund.[15]

One family completed, and another family growing fast. So too was John Bennett's importance in the world of trade and enterprise. At this time, John Bennett is on the board of the Goole Marshland and Howdenshire Pure Tillage and Cattle Food Company Ltd. At their annual general meeting 10th February 1875 held at the Lowther Hotel "Mr J Bennett of Grove House, Goole" is present. The company's financial situation comes under discussion, and they also report on the value of company shares. The cash flow problems experienced by this company, seemed to be brought about by the fact that they would issue credit to their customers until 31st December, even though the goods may have been delivered since the preceding January. Discount incentives are given to try to encourage early settlement of accounts. The account of this meeting in the Goole and Marshland Times Friday 12th February 1875 states:

"Such terms necessitated their having credit at the bank, and their account was usually overdrawn somewhere between £5,000 and £10,000, but yesterday, they had for the first time since the company was formed, a balance of £10 15 11d, to their credit at the bank". It goes on to say "There [sic] £2 shares were now worth, and had been sold at 2/7/6, showing a profit of 7/6 per share." During the meeting it was agreed to pay dividends to shareholders on a half yearly basis, whilst continuing to hold annual meetings as was currently the practice. Details of production were also given at the meeting "At their first annual meeting they had made 1,200 tons of manure, but this year had manufactured over 6,000 tons". It goes on to report "They had only had one complaint from all their customers and that gentleman said he tried three other makes as well and found them all of no good." Obviously it was difficult to satisfy this particular gentleman. The following summary from the meeting shows that profits were marginal. "The accounts showed that on the 6427 tons made, the profit was only £2840, or less than 10/- a ton".

Three weeks later, on 4th March 1875, at the same venue, the Lowther Hotel in Goole, John Bennett attends the annual meeting of shareholders of the Goole Steam Shipping Company Limited. John Bennett is an honourable secretary for the company together with Robert Storr Best and Joseph Barry Hayes. The Goole and Marshland Times, Friday 5th March 1875 states that:

"They were able to declare a div [sic] of 10 per cent, and a bonus of 30/- per share, which was equal to a return of 20 per cent." The newspaper report goes on to say - "During the year they had had two accidents – the burning of one of the ships and the running down by another, - but all were paid fair and square out of the accounts of the year". It is worth pointing out how the absence of insurance in these days would come to affect John Bennett in his own empire in years to come. Fortunately the ability to predict the future had not been invented! Whilst this company was far away from the corridors of parliamentary debate, it is intriguing to note that there was an avenue for their interests to be made known as shown in this excerpt from the meeting – "......great magnates connected with the trade. Mr Stanhope, M.P., though not so frequently with them, had been in common with Lord Houghton of great assistance to them in Parliament and through them to the shipping interest in the country. There was now before the House of Commons a bill affecting that interest, in reference to which it was necessary that their opinion should be duly represented (cheer)." Mr Vickers present at the meeting expressed concern as reported "He thought the reserve fund was hardly large enough for so large a company, they had a capital of £50,000, but their reserve was only £3,000. Now when they had a bad year and lost 6 per cent on the year they were £6,000 out of pocket". He went on to suggest "that they should open out new trades, and hoped the directors would try to do so." Perhaps this would spark an idea in John Bennett's mind about buying his own ship? The meeting agreed to hold this matter in abeyance "but it would still be considered by the directors in the interests of the port and especially of the company (hear, hear)."

It is in the summer of 1875 that Mary Ann Sykes gives birth to Edith Elizabeth, on 30th June 1875 in the district of North Meols, at 4 Leicester Street Southport.[16] Mary Ann registers the birth on the 31st July but does not name the father on the birth certificate. Once again she gives Edith her surname. Similar to East Beach, Lytham, Leicester Street, Southport, is the address of affluent individuals, Doctors, J.P.'s, Merchants and Independents. Most properties, however, were Lodging Houses. In the 1881 census, Charlotte Sorby spinster age 51, described as a Lodging House Keeper, lives at No.4. At the time of this census two 'gentlewomen' are boarding, along with a Bailiff, his wife and servant. It is difficult to say whether this address has any significance. It is intriguing to note that the name 'North Meols' derives from the Scandinavian name meaning 'sand hill'. This is the name of the farmstead occupied by John Bennett before moving to Grove House. Edith would go on to have the nickname "Tiddy".

John decides to buy Mary Ann a better home. On the 6th August 1875, the deed to a property at 9 South Parade Doncaster transfers from John Darley of Doncaster, Gent., to John Bennett.[17] It consists of a dwelling house with yard, garden, stable, outbuildings and out offices. John clearly intends to carry out some of his business from there. The deed also confirms that the property is now occupied by Mrs Sykes. It is interesting to note that John has as his witnesses a Thomas Atkinson solicitor of Doncaster and Arthur James Shirley (clerk to this solicitor). George England, the family solicitor of Goole, was not party to this transaction perhaps to ensure secrecy from his family and friends in Goole. This is probably arranged whilst Mary Ann is away for the birth of Edith Elizabeth. She remained in Southport the previous week as seen above, so must have moved straight into her new home on her return.

John by now has business interests in two key companies, in the town of Goole. With doubtless passion for work, in September 1875, John is embarking on another principle venture, the establishment of the Goole Market Hall Company Limited. The Goole and Marshland Times, of Friday 17th September 1875, reports details of this newly proposed company. The report states that the provisional committee comprises John Bennett, Grove House, Goole; Ralph Creyke,

Rawcliffe Hall; Joseph Barry Hayes, Claughton Villa, Goole; Robert Storr Best, Moorefields, Goole (both seen with John above as honorary secretaries of the Goole Steam Shipping Company); Thomas Huntington, Aire Street, Goole; Thomas Owston, Ebor Terrace, Goole; William Garlick, Field House, Goole. John obviously moves in the same circles as these other prominent men, since their names appear regularly on boards, committees and at meetings. As a merchant and involved in the farming community, John would be well placed to recognise the need for a new Market Hall, within his home town of Goole. The newspaper goes on to report "The town is well and centrally situated in the neighbourhood of a large producing area, from which great quantities of farmers' produce ought to be collected, and since the opening of the North Eastern Railway it has not only convenient access to the great consuming centres, but also to the extensive producing district between Goole and Hull." It was anticipated that the creation of this "commodious market enclosure would at once improve the attendance on Wednesday, and promote the general welfare of the town". The market continues to this time to be held on Wednesday, although the range of goods for sale has changed markedly from those days gone by.

Some useful information about the extent of John Bennett's personal wealth can be seen, as the proposed market hall is to be erected "on a portion of land called Bennett's Town, and adjoining Boothferry Road, - the most rapidly growing part of the town, and about to be most densely populated." The newspaper account goes on to say that "the land contains 2637 square yards". The occupation of this site was to be secured for a period of 99 years. John Bennett and Robert Storr Best (on behalf of this new company) agree to purchase the iron and glass structure formerly used by the Market Hall in Doncaster. Inside the market building there would be "Ten first-rate shops with windows opening on to the Market" which they anticipated would be "a source of profit to the Company". They expect a significant income to be generated from the shops together with rent for stalls on Wednesdays and Saturdays. The Company also plans to make this building suitable as a venue for large public meetings and auctions, from which additional income would be generated. The meeting invites prospective shareholders to apply for shares, and they set a date for a general shareholders meeting to be held on the 20th September. A follow up report in the Goole and Marshland Times the following Friday (24th September 1875) advises that 477 shares are allotted to 82 shareholders, leaving just 23 of the 500 left for allocation. In the same edition of the newspaper, there is also a report of this meeting held on the 20th September. It confirms that the company has been formed with 500 shares of £5 each. There were to be nine directors – Mr Bennett, Mr Rockett, Capt. Best, Messrs Huntington, Burkill, R J Wake, G England, jun., J Moss, jun., W Garlick, E Thompson, and W Pease. The list for some reason includes eleven names. It concludes with the information that "Mr Bennett was elected chairman of the board, and Mr. Haldenby clerk. The registered offices of the company will be at Messrs. England and Son's, East Parade, Goole."

So John acquires another prominent position. This account shows that, at this time, John Bennett has offices at Railway Dock in Goole. It is evident from these three newspaper accounts alone, that John is a significant player in the business community, and a man moving in circles of like-minded men, who could recognise business opportunities when they came along. At the age of 39, he was clearly not a man to sit back on his laurels.

Like many entrepreneurs, John also plays a key role in the social welfare of his community. He is a member of the Goole and Hook Sanitary Committee, and on the Tuesday following, the 21st September 1875, is chairing a meeting of this committee. At this meeting, various nuisances and matters of health and the environment are discussed. These range from the removal of pigsties in St.John Street; the offensive state of the drain behind George Street in Old Goole; to the poor quality of water bored from Boothferry Road. One amusing point from the report is the claim received from a Mrs Morris who has destroyed infected bedding on the instructions of the Sanitary Officer. Having carried out these instructions to the letter, she then wishes to claim 20/- (20 shillings) to cover their value. The committee decide to investigate this matter further. One has to be impressed that someone clearly as busy as John finds time to participate in such a committee, also having the patience to try to educate certain individuals (through enforced regulations) in matters affecting their own health.

Less than a month after the above newspaper report, the local news section of the Goole and Marshland Times, on Friday 15th October 1875, announces that "We understand that Mr John Bennett has been appointed chairman of the Goole Engineering and Shipbuilding Company, Limited." This is yet another key position of responsibility in what would have been a very busy organisation for the port of Goole at that time. Also in the same edition is the first appearance of this advertisement (*figure 16*).

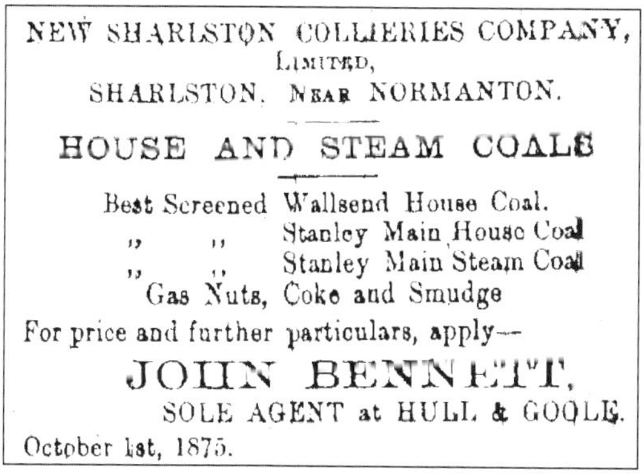

NEW SHARLSTON COLLIERIES COMPANY,
LIMITED,
SHARLSTON. NEAR NORMANTON.

HOUSE AND STEAM COALS

Best Screened Wallsend House Coal.
    ,,   ,,   Stanley Main House Coal
    ,,   ,,   Stanley Main Steam Coal
    Gas Nuts, Coke and Smudge
For price and further particulars, apply--

JOHN BENNETT,
SOLE AGENT at HULL & GOOLE.
October 1st, 1875.

Figure 16

During his early business years as a merchant and importer, John Bennett has the idea that instead of sending the ships he charters across to France loaded with ballast, he could profit enormously by filling them with a cargo in demand by his French counterparts. This cargo was to be 'Black Gold' or more commonly known as 'coal'. John Bennett is trading in house and steam coals, being the sole agent for this company at the ports of Hull and Goole. He is also hiring vessels to deliver coal and potatoes across to France. Albert Chatelle writes:

"Those were still the good old days when the Boulogne Newspapers were informing our Grandmothers that the firm of Bennett b.e. Langlett and that of Mr Fred Harwyn Belle, 8 Quai Basin Loubet were offering screened coal from Goole at 30 francs per metric ton which then seemed dear but Mr Ludovic Dufoles, Coal Merchant, on the Navarin market was selling to all corners at 20 francs per ton delivered to houses even outside the town".

Never being long out of the newspapers the name of John Bennett appears again in the edition of the Goole and Marshland Times the following week on Friday 22nd October 1875 – *figure 17*.

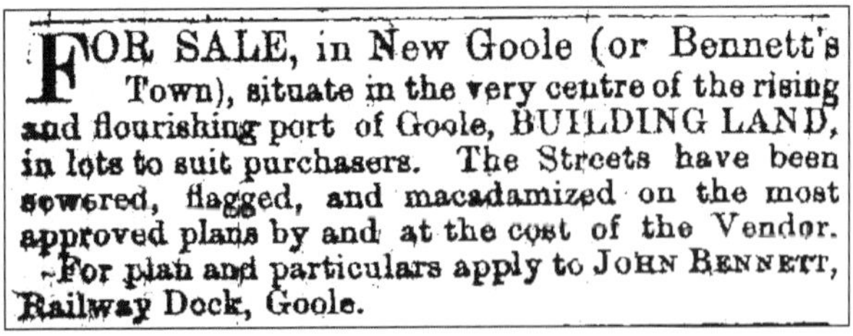

FOR SALE, in New Goole (or Bennett's Town), situate in the very centre of the rising and flourishing port of Goole, BUILDING LAND, in lots to suit purchasers. The Streets have been sewered, flagged, and macadamized on the most approved plans by and at the cost of the Vendor. For plan and particulars apply to JOHN BENNETT, Railway Dock, Goole.

Figure 17

Since the purchase, the previous year, John is now ready to start selling the land. Perhaps he is trying to raise some capital to begin his next venture? As already seen, John is to make some of this land available for the newly proposed market hall. The next chapter shows some of the sale transactions.

Just a week after that report, John Bennett is in the newspaper again embarking on yet another venture. In the Goole and Marshland Times of Friday 29th October 1875, a list of persons nominated for the new Goole Local Board is published: "BENNETT, John, merchant, Grove House; nom:

T. Kendall, G.Sutton, W.W.Hunter". Those nominating John are themselves also nominated: "KENDALL, Thos., agent for the A[ire] & C[alder] Navigation; nom: J. Bennett, W.W. Hunter," and "HUNTER, W.W., tailor, Bank Buildings; nom: G. Hewson." The report states "It will be seen there have been 90 nominations, the number of persons nominated being 58". They were vying for nine places on the board. Again the same familiar names of those within the social circle come up; Robert Storr Best, Thomas Huntington, and Joseph Barry Hayes. The list includes key figures of the town and district, traders, farmers, ship-owner, shipbuilders, surgeons, hoteliers etc. This election stirred up quite a deal of fuss about the suitability of those nominated to the proposed positions. There was a keen interest in "introducing new blood into the new local board" (Goole and Marshland Times, Friday 29th October 1875 in a report on a "Meeting of Mr.Hickman's Supporters"). In another (anonymous) letter, to the editor published in the same edition the author writes "It will be unwise in the extreme to elect men of straw; that have not got a yard of land, or property in the district, or men you may term as birds of passage; here today and gone tomorrow". Another avid onlooker writes in his letter (published in the same edition) appealing to the electorate "that they will carefully avoid doing two things; first, giving votes to those who because they are on all the Boards well nigh in the town and district, cannot reasonably be expected to devote sufficient time to the heavy business of the Local Board; second, giving votes to those who, through the whole of their connection with public business, are well known to having stood in the way of necessary public improvements". How would John Bennett's character have been viewed? He was certainly a busy man, but who can say how passionately he may have taken his responsibility? Another letter writer who signs himself "A Well-Wisher" declares "We want men who have general interest in property in the town, and who have good, social positions, that the health and comfort and advancement of the inhabitants can be properly represented."

In the space of eight months in 1875, John Bennett is described as a merchant and is also owner of a substantial area of land – Bennett's Town – into which he has already invested heavily by installing the service infrastructure. He is with the Pure Tillage and Cattle Food Company Limited, chairman of the newly formed Goole Market Hall Company Limited, also a member of the Goole and Hook Sanitary Committee. John, recently becoming a coal merchant, has offices at Railway Dock, Goole. Appointed chairman of the Goole Steam Shipping Company Limited, he is also standing for election to the new Goole Local Board. Remember that, at this point, he is also the father of twelve children. Clearly an extremely busy man!

A new Act of Parliament comes into force around this time, to prevent unseaworthy ships from leaving port. With John Bennett's next business venture just around the corner, one can assume that this would certainly have caught his attention.

Goole and Marshland Times, Friday, 29th October 1875

UNSEAWORTHY SHIPS

"The Act of Parliament passed during last session for the purpose of giving further powers to the Board of Trade to stop unseaworthy ships will come into operation on Monday next. At present, we believe, the Board of Trade has not exercised the power conferred upon it by the new Act, of appointing a number of persons with power to detain unseaworthy vessels, there being, no doubt, in most ports, as in Hull, already a sufficient staff of officers to carry on the work. When appointed, such officers will have the same power as inspectors appointed by the Board of Trade under the Merchant Shipping Act, and any interference with them in the discharge of their duties will render the offender liable to the penalties now imposed under the same Act. If one fourth of the crew of any vessel duly complain that the vessel is unseaworthy, the Board of Trade will be bound to detain the ship for the purpose of surveying. In future no vessel will be allowed to carry more than one third of her cargo in any kind of grain, unless such cargo be contained in sacks or barrels, or be secured from shifting; and any captain of a British ship violating this section of the Act will be liable to a penalty not exceeding £200. The penalties imposed under the 11th section of the Merchant Shipping Act of 1874 are repealed, and in lieu thereof several classes of offences are specified which become misdemeanour. Any person sending a ship to sea in an unseaworthy state, and the owner of such vessel are both guilty of misdemeanour. Any person even attempting to do so, and the master knowingly taking such vessel out to sea will also be guilty of misdemeanour. Any owner failing to register at the custom-house the name and address of the managing owner of a British ship will be liable to a penalty of £500 each time that ship leaves any port in the United Kingdom unregistered. Under this section, no prosecution can be instituted except with the consent of the Board of Trade. The position of the various decks of a ship above water is to be conspicuously and permanently marked with lines not less than one inch broad and 12 inches long, painted longitudinally on the sides of the vessels amidships. The new principle of making the maximum load-line will be by painting a disc 12 inches in diameter with a horizontal line 18 inches long drawn through its centre. The centre of the disc will be the load-line in salt water. The owner must before going out of the port deliver to the officer of customs a written statement of the distance between the centre, of the disc and the ship's decks above that centre, and in default of making this statement the officer of customs may refuse to enter the ship outwards. Any owner or master neglecting thus to mark his ship shall for each offence be liable to a penalty not exceeding £100. In all contracts of service between the ship-owners and the crews of vessels, all reasonable efforts to ensure the seaworthiness of the ship from the commencement to the close of the voyage are understood to be made, whether mentioned or not. It is somewhat singular that although the

Act clearly points out how the load-line is to be marked it does not give specific instructions as to the detention of the vessels if it is too deep in the water. Probably it is thought that the Board of Trade has already sufficient power to prevent such a ship going to sea.

In anticipation of the operation of the Act, most of the regular trading vessels of this port have the deck line and the disc placed upon their sides, and no doubt before the end of the present week all vessels will be so marked. It may be mentioned that the position of this load line is not fixed by Act of Parliament, but it is left to each owner to say, by the painting on a load-line, to what draught of water he intends to load his vessel. The Act does not apply to fishing vessels and to river craft."

With land sales going very well, and presumably his income increasing satisfactorily, John Bennett is about to hit the high seas!

Chapter 4
A Shipping Magnate is Born

In the 'Local News' published in the Goole and Marshland Times Friday 5th November 1875, it is announced:

NEW STEAMER.—Within the last few days Mr. John Bennett has become the possessor of the ss Plover, a steamer of 270 tons, with which he intends to trade between Goole and the continent. The Plover is a new boat.

Figure 18

It is not quite true that this is a new boat since it was built in 1873, by Blake of Norfleet, with engines by Millwall DK of London. This ship is sold in 1876 to the Co-Operative Wholesale Society of Goole, who subsequently sells it to a Norwegian company in 1880. The Plover owned by W Liddell of London first appears in Lloyds Register, in 1874, and then again in 1875. John Bennett then purchases it as seen in the above newspaper report.

Although a steamer of modest proportions, nevertheless this is a new vessel for John Bennett, and one wonders if the capital expected to be raised from the sale of Bennett's Town would allow bankers to provide John with the capital required to purchase this. On the other hand, John may well have had sufficient income to purchase his vessel without the help of his bank manager. *Figure 19* shows some of the specification details of the Plover, taken from Lloyds Register. The shipping list in the newspaper of the following week shows her arrival into Goole on the 4th November 1875. She is under the command of Captain Heywood and brings a cargo of

Figure 19

Ship No	68480
Name	Plover
Description	Iron Screw Schooner
Tonnage	124 net 208 gross 161 under deck
Dimensions	Length – 119.8 Breadth – 19.6 Depth – 9.7
Engines	CI2Cy11.5" & 20"-18" 30 HP By Millwall DK of E W London
Builder	Blake of Norfleet
Built	1873
Owner	John Bennett
Registered port	Goole

timber from London. The entrepreneurial Mr Bennett is taking full advantage of the trip, assuming of course this is his cargo. With typical business acumen, John wastes no time in firing up steam, and his new vessel sets out two days later on the 6th November, under the command of a Captain Redford with a cargo described as 'goods' bound for Rotterdam.

At the beginning of 1876, John is selling his plots at 'Bennett's Town'. On the 6th January, 1,678 square yards (plots 66, 67, 68 and 68a) sold to William Sleight Auctioneer.[18] On 9th May 1876, 1,187 square yards (plots 21 & 22 on the general plan of the estate) sold in a group purchase. The various individuals buying this land are William Eden Cass, surgeon; William Porter Rank, agent; William Simpson, shipwright; Thomas Hitchman, whitesmith; George Stewart, slater; and Joseph Cawthorn, commission agent; all of Goole. William Johnston, hosier; Thomas Johnston, draper; John Wright, dock dues collector; Charles Whitee Holdich, boot seller; William Hudson, docker; Thomas Stratton, merchant; all of Hull.[19]

Another vessel built in 1873 is the ss Hydra, under special survey and registered class 90A1. When it first appears in Lloyds Register, in 1874, the owners are Jobson Bros of Newcastle. In the following year, the owners listed are Jobson Bros of Newcastle and J Bennett of Goole. Surveys of the vessel take place in April 1874 at Newcastle and then in October 1875 at Falmouth. In 1876, John Bennett is the sole owner. *Figure 20* shows a photograph of the Hydra, and the specification from the 1876 register appears in *figure 21*.

John Bennett establishes a regular steamship service between Goole and Calais. Shortly afterwards he commences a Goole to Ostend service of steamers. The service to Calais only continued for some twelve months, and in 1876, this French port changed to Boulogne-sur-Mer, a harbour possessing greater opportunities for the building up of a profitable service than that of Calais. The Calais operation had only one sailing a week each way; the Boulogne service requires two sailings each way weekly. John Bennett's Red Cross Line is born. The company's house flag is white with a broad blue border and red cross in the centre. A naming convention is soon established with all the chosen names for vessels ending with 'a'. The flag can be seen on the glass panel (from the Goole office) now displayed in Goole museum.

Also in this year, John Bennett commissions the construction of a new steamer, the ss India, from Readheads of South Shields. The official year of build is 1876. The registered ship number is 67820 and her gross tonnage given as 368. A photograph of the vessel can be seen in *figure 23*. A notice (transcribed in *figure 22*) appears in The Goole and Marshland Weekly Times of 13th October 1876 announcing his purchase. The India appears in Lloyds Register of 1877. *Figure 24* shows the specification details. A survey of the India takes place in South Shields in October 1876, then again in Goole in May 1877. Also found in the same edition of the newspaper, is the fact that John Bennett is now one of the Vice

Figure 20

Figure 21

Ship No	67388
Name	Hydra
Description	Iron Screw Schooner
Master	J Ingleby
Tonnage	245 net 393 gross 372 under deck
Dimensions	Length – 154.7 Breadth – 23.8 Depth – 13.8
Engines	CI2Cy18.5" & 36"-24" 6olb 50 HP By Pattinson & Atkinson, Newcastle
Builder	Lindsay of Newcastle
Built	1873
Owner	John Bennett
Registered port	Goole
Port of survey	Fal [Falmouth] A & CP
Class	90 A1

"NEW STEAMER – We have before alluded to the enterprise shown by
Mr. John Bennett, of Grove House, in the establishment of a new trade
between Ostend and Calais, and Goole. To the Plover and Hydra, which
have been running for about a year, he has added the India, a fine vessel
which arrived on Sunday from South Shields, where she has been built by
Messrs Redhead and Son. The India is a well-built vessel, carefully
designed for the purpose of accomplishing the voyage between Goole and
Ostend within 24 hours. Her dimensions are 160 feet between the
perpendiculars, 20 feet beam and 12 feet 6 inches of hold. She is classed
100 A1 at Lloyds, and has been provided with engines of 70 horse power.
She will load to 520 tons being specially adapted for trade for which she is
intended, and being also fitted with all the latest improvements in
reference to machinery, accommodations for her crew, & c Her draught
is 12 feet 5 inches and 12 foot 3 inches aft. We wish her a successful career
and trust as trade improves our merchants and companies may make
further efforts to meet the requirements of the trade to and from Goole.
Captain Ingleby is to command the India."

Figure 22

presidents of the Goole Chamber of Commerce and Shipping.
They have just held their monthly meeting where he acts as
Chair, and they discuss the matter of postal deliveries in the
town:

"The monthly meeting of the directors of this body was held
on Friday, present – Mr.Bennett (one of the vice-presidents)
in the chair, Messrs Lyth, J E Porter and Bray. The secretary
laid upon the table a copy of the catalogue of the British
section of the Philadelphia International Exhibition, which
had been received from the Duke of Richmond and Gordon.
The Chairman brought forward the question of the delivery of
letters in Old Goole, complaints having being made that while
the rest of the town had an afternoon delivery Old Goole had
none. This was not so much of an inconvenience to the
merchants residing there, as they had private boxes at the
post office, but to the other residents, many of whom were
mariners, and their families. The directors thought that Old
Goole should have an afternoon delivery, and though not in
favour of increasing the labours of the post-office on Sunday,
yet that the whole town should be put on the same footing in

Figure 23

Figure 24

Ship No	67820
Name	India
Description	Iron Screw Schooner
Master	J Ingleby
Tonnage	230 net 368 gross 347 under deck
Dimensions	Length – 160.0 Breadth – 23.8 Depth – 12.5
Engines	CI2Cy20" & 38"-26" 65lb 70 HP By Redhead & Co, South Shields
Builder	Redhead & Co, South Shields
Built	1876
Owner	John Bennett
Registered port	Goole
Port of survey	Shl [Shields?] A & CP Goo [Goole] Double bottom 75ft
Class	100 A1

reference to the delivery of letters in the morning of that day. It was also stated that telegrams were charged 6d extra in some parts of Old Goole, as portions of that district were more than a mile from the old post-office. This charge it was also considered should be removed. The secretary was instructed to bring these matters before the post-office authorities, with a view to their being properly adjusted, so that all parts of the town might be treated in the same manner and enjoy the same facilities in reference to the receipt and despatch of telegrams and letters. Mr J.E.Porter gave notice that at the next meeting he would bring forward the question of the appointment of a German canon at Goole. The matter had been mooted before and it would be well if the hands of private parties were strengthened by the influence of the Chamber."

No doubt, living himself in Old Goole, John would perhaps have felt aggrieved at receiving post once daily. One can imagine his post bag being quite full!

As mentioned earlier, John sells the Plover in 1876 to the Co-Operative Wholesale Society of Goole. On the 1st March 1877, a 'Memorandum Agreement' details a joint venture between the Society and John Bennett to continue until 31st December 1879.[20] The agreement is that the Society will use their ship the Plover, with John Bennett using both of his ships at the time, the Hydra and India. All three ships will then be operated as a joint service and business enterprise by John Bennett. The Society will advance £1000 for facilitating the business and promoting the service and John Bennett will put £2000 into the operation. The Society will make available another steamer of not less than 550 tons and 65-70 horsepower before 1st September 1877. Each party is responsible for maintaining/repairing or replacing their own vessels, however, John Bennett is also responsible for stocking and insuring all three vessels. The Society will pay the fee of £4 for clearing each vessel for each voyage. John Bennett will act as the Forwarding Agent for the Society. The

Society is to receive one equal third part of the net profit from the service, whilst John Bennett is to receive five percent on the amount of all gross sea freight. All coal is to be purchased directly from the pits. The final stipulation is that the name of the Co-Operative Wholesale Society will not appear in connection with the service.

According to Albert Chatelle, the India arrives for the first time at Boulogne on 30th March 1877. Shipping lists show that the India returns to Goole on the 6th and 20th April and the 4th and 17th May 1877, and, from then, a regular service continues.

More 'Bennett's Town' property transactions go through in this year. On 1st May approximately 2005 square yards of land between Stanley and Estcourt Streets, transfers by deed to George Middlewood a builder of 5 Alexander Road, Moss Side, Manchester.[21] Also registered on 1st May 1877 is an Indenture to transfer a deed of property close to South and Back South Streets in Goole.[22] This transfer is between The Goole Engineering and Shipbuilding Company (1st part), John Bennett of Grove House (2nd part), Marmaduke Storr Hodson of Leeds, Gent and Agent of Trustees for Undertakers of Navigation of Rivers Aire and Calder (3rd part), to Thomas Scott of Hollybank, Claughton, Cheshire, a Civil Engineer (4th part). The property in question is 788 square yards of land bounded by Barge Dock Wharf to the north, South Street to the south, land leased to Robert Briggs on the west, and premises of the above Trustees to the east. It included foundries, blacksmith shop, sheds, boiler house and other buildings built by John Pilkington.

Almost a year to the day later, news is reported of another new addition to the Bennett fleet, the ss China, in the Goole and Marshland Weekly Times on Friday, October 19th 1877. A transcription of this notice appears in *figure 25*. The China's registered ship number is 67824. John Bennett, obviously satisfied with the India, orders the China from Redheads.

"A NEW STEAMER FOR GOOLE – This week we have to chronicle the launch of another fine new steamer, which is to run between here and Boulogne in connection with the line of Mr John Bennett is the owner. A vessel – which was named the China – was launched a few days ago from the yard of Messrs. Redhead and Son of South Shields, and she will be with all despatch, rigged, equipped and prepared for sea, so that she will be ready to sail for Boulogne on her first voyage early in November. Her measurement is 580 tons dead weight, her engines are of 80 horse power and she will be classed at Lloyds 100 a. Capt. Ingleby, late of the India, will be put in command of her and her chief engineer will be Mr. Spilman."

Figure 25

Perhaps he commissioned the two ships together? John Bennett gives charge of this vessel to Captain Ingleby who was previously in command of the India. *Figure 26* shows the China, built 1877. *Figure 27* gives the ship's specification from Lloyd's Register. The newspapers of the time report all ships movements, and in the 'Shipping List' appearing in The Goole and Marshland Weekly Times the following week, 26th October 1877, are two vessels belonging to John Bennett and the Plover he is operating for the Co-operative Wholesale Society.

GOOLE SHIPPING
Arrived –
Oct 18 India ss, Powell, goods, Boulogne.
....
21 Hydra, ss, Woodhead, goods, Boulogne
....
23 Plover, ss, Gill, goods, Dunkirk

Sailed -
20, India, ss, Powell, goods, Boulogne
.....
21, Hydra, ss, Woodhead, goods, Ostend

Figure 26

Figure 27

Ship No	67824
Name	China
Description	Iron Screw Schooner
Master	J Ingleby
Tonnage	291 net 467 gross 376 under deck
Dimensions	Length – 169.60 Breadth – 25.7 Depth – 12.2
Engines	CI2Cy22" & 40"-27" 70lb 80 HP By Redhead & Co, South Shields
Builder	Redhead & Co, South Shields
Built	1877
Owner	John Bennett
Registered port	Goole
Port of survey	Shl [Shields?] A & CP Goo [Goole] Double Bottom 82ft
Class	100 A1 (built under special survey)

The China has yet to sail. The India, now under the charge of a Captain Powell, can be seen taking 'goods' to and from Boulogne. On this date, the Hydra, under the command of Captain Woodhead, arrives from Boulogne with goods, leaving the same day (on the return tide) bound for Ostend also loaded with goods. John Bennett's company, Red Cross Line, is trading from offices at Railway Dock, Goole, and 'Quai Bonaparte', Boulogne at this time.

The same newspaper reports that John Bennett attends a meeting of the Goole & Marshland Chamber of Agriculture, held at the Lowther Hotel, Goole. At this meeting, the Chamber discusses whether they should set the statute hiring dates, to which they agree. They also agree that they should have a central chamber of agriculture with the suggested location being York.

Towards the end of 1877, more 'Bennett's Town' land sales take place. 1334 square yards (lot 19 and part of lot 20) transfer by deed on 5th December, to George Shearbourne Joiner of Goole.[23]

On the 3rd September 1878, the country witnessed the greatest disaster in the history of coastal cruising when PS Princess Alice sank after a collision at Galleons Reach on the Thames close to Woolwich. Having left Swan Pier near London Bridge, the paddle steamer was on a routine trip to Gravesend and Sheerness packed with day trippers many of whom were visiting Rosherville Gardens. On her return just before 8.00 in the evening, and almost at North Woolwich Pier (where most of the passengers would disembark), the Bywell Castle (a steam collier of 890 tons) steamed towards her. After confusion over their manoeuvre to pass, the Bywell Castle hit the paddle steamer cutting her in two. She sank in four minutes. Many passengers went down with the vessel. The passengers that do not drown with the vessel found themselves in the polluted river near the North Outfall sewer. Almost 700 lost their lives; around 120 bodies unidentified.

This must have been an enormous tragedy and particularly noted in the world of shipping. The Board of Trade enquiry recommended that two vessels under steam should always 'pass each other on the port side'. New rules for navigating the Thames came into force in 1880. These also included reducing the number of passengers ships could carry, and increasing the number of lifebelts vessels had to provide for their passengers. No doubt John Bennett would have been well aware of the tragedy and all the recommendations that came about as a result of it. His vessels would soon be using the Thames. The masters on Bennetts' ships in 1878/9 have changed slightly now; the Hydra, Powell; the China, Thomas Woodhead; the India, John Ingleby. It is highly likely that John Bennett briefed all of the captains on these new regulations.

Coming back to the family, John Bentley Bennett (known to the family as 'Jack') arrives 3rd October 1878, the youngest son to John and Mary Ann, his birth registered at Southport.

A ship that will eventually be owned by John Bennett is also built at this time, although this is for another operator. The shipbuilder W B Thompson of Dundee launches the steamship "Berlin", in 1879 (*figure 28*), that they had built for the Yorkshire Coal and Steamship Co., Goole. Built of iron, the Berlin is 700 tons gross and 130 horse power. Her registered number is 67827. Thompson set up the Tay Foundry in Maryfield then began his business as a shipbuilder in 1874. His business operated from the Caledon Yard, and the first vessel he built was for the fourth Earl of Caledon of Caledon Castle, Tyrone. In the early 1880s, he re-opened the old ship yard at Whiteinch near Glasgow. He ran this together with the Caledon Yard and his Tay Foundry for several years. Among the first to adopt mild steel as a new ship-building material[24] Thompsons also built the HMS Hearty promptly requisitioned for the British Navy in 1884 due to her remarkable turn of speed. The Berlin first appears in Lloyds Register, in 1880. The specification can be seen in *figure 29*.

John Bennett has now established strong Anglo–French trading with his steamships. Albert Chatelle gives an indication of the impact the service provided by John Bennett had on the amount of cargo passing through Boulogne for England. He writes:

"In 1877... there passed ....for England 455,000 kgs fruit, 258,000 kgs vegetables and 1,689,000 potatoes. In 1881 approximately 6 years after the ...first steamer chartered by Bennetts they loaded at Boulogne 2,635,000 kgs fruit, 1,682,000 kgs vegetables and 4,670,000 kgs potatoes."

Kelly's Trade Directory of 1881 lists John Bennett under the 'commercial' section as:

"*steam ship owner and general forwarding agent, importer of foreign produce, coal fitter and general merchant; regular steamers for Ostend and Boulogne*".

He is also listed under the 'private resident' section:
"*Bennett, John, Grove House, Old Goole*"

Also in the 'Official Establishments, Local Institutions, etc' section:

"*Bennett's Red Cross Line; office, Railway Dock, steamers India, Hydra & China. To Boulogne, Wed & Sat returning Wed & Sat, to Ostend, Sat returning Wed.*"

Figure 28

Figure 29

Ship No	67827
Name	Berlin
Description	Screw Schooner
Master	C Ayre
Tonnage	452 net 708 gross 542 under deck
Dimensions	Length – 202.3 Breadth – 28.0 Depth – 13.0
Engines	CI2Cy30" & 54"-33" 70lb 130 HP By W B Thompson, Dundee
Builder	W B Thompson, Dundee
Built	1879
Owner	Yorkshire Coal & Steam Ship Co (Lim)
Registered port	Goole
Port of survey	Hull Double Bottom 104ft
Class	90 A1

The following photographs, from an album belonging to John Bennett, show the family around this time. *Figure 30* is a picture of John Bennett at an age estimated between 30 and 40 years, placing him at about the time in this story. *Figure 31*, believed to be Mary Ann Sykes, taken around a similar time to the photograph above. The photographer is F. Whaley of Regent House, Doncaster who was a professional portrait photographer and a successful exhibitor. *Figure 32*, from the same album, is a picture of the same woman with her children. In *figure 33*, the family group photograph appears that it could be the same children a few years later (two boys and two girls) with the addition of a younger child who could be of either sex judging by the clothing. The two girls certainly seemed to have developed the same facial characteristics.

Looking at the 1881 census, the Bennett household is living at Grove House, Goole (*figure 37*). The two eldest sons and fourth son, living in the family home. The third son, Robert aged 16, is a passenger on board one of Bennetts' steamships, the China (*figure 38*). Perhaps Robert is leaving for France. Twelve crew members plus the ship's master, Captain John Ingleby, are also on board. The Bennett girls, it appears, are not at home at this time. Further investigation found them all at the Belvedere Ladies School in Harrogate (*figure 40*). This was quite unusual in some ways, with the girls given a formal education, whilst the boys would seemingly be coached for the family business in clerks' positions. Maybe, on the other hand, it was fashionable for successful business men to equip their daughters with the necessary life skills to marry well. Belvedere House still exists at 2, Victoria Avenue in Harrogate (*figure 34*).

A plaque on the wall adjacent to the building has the following information:

"Victoria Avenue -
The work of the Victoria Park Company in joining the two ancient villages of High and Low Harrogate to form a modern

Figure 30   *Figure 31*

Figure 32   *Figure 33*

town reached a climax in 1860 with the opening of Victoria Avenue. Two of the first developments were The Belvidere [sic] of 1861, now the College of Arts, and the Congregational Church by Lockwood & Mawson of 1861-2. The avenue at one time had private entrance gates and the combination of wide roads and pavements, grass verges, trees and noble buildings provided an example from which future generations could obtain inspiration. Harrogate Borough Council, 1983"[25]

Mrs Ann Moody Potter runs the school in 1881, and, from 1882-3, her husband the Rev. E Potter is in charge. The 1881 census shows this couple resident at 123 Trafalgar Square, Morley Hotel, St.Martin-in-the-Fields, London. Both their son, John M Potter aged 18, and daughter Mary E Potter, were residing in the school. The photograph in *figure 35* depicts the Belvedere and the Congregational Church with the 'Stray' in the foreground, taken 1880. The audience is enjoying a band playing on the Stray. It would not have been unusual for the Bennett girls to have been in this audience. The census also shows who was on board the Hydra on the night of the 3rd of April (*figure 39*); the Ship's master Captain Samuel Wadsworth plus twelve crew members. John's 'second family' can be seen on the 1881 census (*figure 41*) still living at 9 South Parade, Doncaster. The Doncaster map (*figure 36)* shows the location of this street. South Parade was a more affluent area than that at Cartwright Street, where Mary Ann has previously resided. In fact, South Parade would be one of the first streets to receive electricity towards the end of the 19th century. Mary (unlike Sarah Ann) has all her young family at home. Her sister Emily Eleanor Sykes resides in the household in the capacity of governess. Whether paid for her services cannot be confirmed, but it is quite likely that John would ensure this household has everything it requires financially. The fact that Mary Ann has both a cook, Emma Hartley, and a housemaid, Mary Smith to attend to her every need, demonstrates this point. Sarah Ann did not have her own cook (at least not living in), although she did have two general servants.

Figure 34

Figure 35

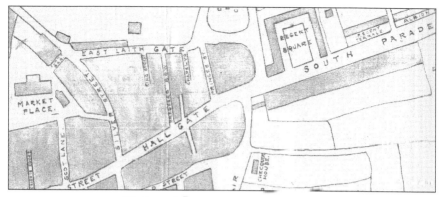

Figure 36 Doncaster map 1872

Mary Ann and John Bennett's youngest daughter Mary Eleanor (known as Mopsy) has not been born at this point.

On Sunday 31st July 1881, an immense fire destroys ten large sheds on the eastern side of the Railway Dock. This must have caused some considerable disruption to the movement of goods in and out of the port. Just short of a hundred years later, I remember standing as a young child on the banks of the Dutch River watching a massive warehouse fire blazing out of control on the docks.

The following year 1882 sees the opening of the Aldam dock in Goole. The excavation of this dock cuts off the Aire Street station of the LYR railway.

On the 2nd April 1883 John Bennett drafts his will.[26] Various facts about John's business and private life are evident. To his wife Sarah Ann he bequeaths: "I give all my plate linen china glass books pictures wines liquors consumable articles furniture and other household effects to my said wife Sarah Ann Bennett absolutely" He also gives her the sum of £50 upon his death, and the income generated from Highfields Farm. However, he also bequeaths to Mary Ann Sykes £50 upon his death, and the income from a farm occupied by Thomas Johnson (assumed to be a tenant). So the two women are both provided for. The will mentions all of John and Sarah

Figure 37 – Census 1881 – Goole

Abode	Person	Relationship To Head Of Family	Cond*	Age Male	Age Female	Rank, Profession Or Occupation	Where Born
Grove House, Marshland Road, Goole	John Bennett	Head	Mar	45		Land & Steamship Owner	Yorkshire, Adlingfleet
	Sarah Bennett	Wife	Mar		38	Wife	Lincolnshire, Crowle
	John Bennett	Son	U	19		Commercial Clerk	Yorkshire, Adlingfleet
	Herbert Bennett	Son	U	17		Commercial Clerk	Yorkshire, Adlingfleet
	Albert Bennett	Son	U	7		Scholar	Yorkshire, Goole
	Mary Greaves	Servant	U		19	General Servant Domestic	Yorkshire, Rawcliffe
	Elizabeth Pycott	Servant	U		18	General Servant Domestic	Lincolnshire, Crowle

*Condition Mar=Married U=Unmarried

Figure 38 Census 1881 – Goole (following image)

Abode	Person	Relationship To Head	Cond*	Age Male	Age Female	Rark, Prof. Or Occ.	Where Born
SS China	John Ingleby		M	52		Master (Seaman)	Leeds, York
	Thomas Woodhead		M	40		Mate (Seaman)	Selby, York
	William Denby		M	25		Second Mate (Seaman)	Wisbeach, Cambridge
	George Rainley		M	33		Cook (Seaman)	Rawcliffe, York
	Richard Risebury		M	29		Able Seaman	Willes, Norfolk
	Thomas Wright		M	33		Able Seaman	Willes, Norfolk
	Edward Lynn		M	46		Able Seaman	Goole, York
	William Watson		U	26		Able Seaman	Goole, York
	John Thresh		M	37		Able Seaman	Doncaster, York
	George Webster		M	27		Chief Engineer	Boston, Lincoln
	David Mathers		U	32		Second Engineer	Auchinblee, Scotland
	James Dawson		M	48		Fireman	North Cave, York
	Alfred Wilson		U	25		Fireman	Sandy, Cambs
	Robert Bennett		U	16		Passenger Scholar	Adlingfleet

*Condition M=Married U=Unmarried

Figure 39 Census 1881 – Goole

Abode	Person	Relationship To Head	Cond*	Age		Rank, Prof. Or Occ.	Where Born
				Male	Female		
SS Hydra	Samuel Wadsworth		M	38		Master (Seaman)	Brotherton, York
	Eli Alcock		M	45		Mate (Seaman)	Lincoln, England
	Edwin Foster		U	25		Second Mate (Seaman)	Goole, York, England
	Frederick Burch		M	39		Steward Seaman	Woodbridge, Suffolk
	Samuel Asquith		M	31		Able Seaman	Pontefract, York
	William Freear		M	48		Able Seaman	Crowle, Lincoln
	Richard Norton		M	34		Able Seaman	Hull, York
	John Wright		M	43		Able Seaman	Selby, York
	William Spilman		M	50		Chief Engineer	Whitton, Lincoln
	Thomas Jackson		U	25		Second Engineer	Goole, York
	William Hardwick		M	32		Fireman	Goole, York
	James Laverack		M	26		Fireman	Swinefleet, York
	George William Hudson		U	23		Fireman	Manchester, Lancs

*Condition   M=Married   U=Unmarried

Figure 40 Excerpt from Census 1881 – Bilton cum Harrogate

Abode	Person	Relationship To Head	Cond*	Age		Rank, Prof. Or Occ.	Where Born
				Male	Female		
Belvedere Ladies School	......						
	......						
	Sarah A Bennett				10	Scholar	Landhill [sic]Yorkshire
	Mary A Bennett				12	Scholar	Landhill [sic]Yorkshire
	Annie C Bennett				14	Scholar	Landhill [sic]Yorkshire
	......						
	......						
*Condition							

Figure 41 – Census 1881 – Doncaster

Abode	Person	Relationship To Head Of Family	Cond *	Age		Rank, Profession Or Occupation	Where Born
				Male	Female		
9 South Parade, Doncaster	Mary A Sykes	Head	W		35		Luddington, Lincs
	Arthur F Sykes	Son	U	9		Scholar	Doncaster, Yorkshire
	Isabel Sykes	Dau	U		7	Scholar	Lytham, Lancs
	Edith E Sykes	Dau	U		5	Scholar	Southport, Lancs
	John Sykes	Son	U	3		Scholar	Southport, Lancs
	Emily E Sykes	Sister	U		22	Governess	Howden, Yorkshire
	Emma Hartley	Servant	U		23	Cook	Lofthouse, Yorkshire
	Mary Smith	Servant	U		17	Housemaid	Edlington, Yorkshire

*Condition   W=Widow   U=Unmarried

62

Ann's children, but also mentions all of Mary Ann's children, without making reference to the fact that John was their father. One can imagine how curious the solicitor would be with this information unless, of course, he was aware of the circumstances. John, not surprisingly, also bequeaths 9 South Parade, Doncaster, where Mary Ann and their children live, to her upon his death. He also instructs that if Mary Ann dies, the farm mentioned previously is to be sold and the proceeds divided amongst her children. To his children with Sarah Ann, he instructs that they are each to be paid £50 per annum from the age of 21 from his estate. The will also names John's eldest son, John together with William Frank as Executors and Trustees. The will shows that William Frank is now Manager and cashier for the Bennett Company, at Goole and receives £150 per annum in this capacity. He was witness to many of the 'transfer of property' deeds when he was at that time a commercial clerk. Perhaps John was prompted to make his will as his elderly mother Hannah of Keyfield House, Swinefleet, dies intestate on September 7th, aged 78. She outlived her husband Thomas Bennett by 24 years. No doubt John helped his mother financially during her widowhood. She left a personal estate of only £189 15s, and the administration of the estate granted at Wakefield to her son John.[27]

Keyfield House was just one of the properties owned by John Bennett by 1885. He had three of his properties valued by T H Bentley (possibly a relative) of Knottingly 2nd February 1885. The full description of all land and contents of High Field Farm, Mount Pleasant Farm, and Key Field Farm appear in a small maroon leather bound book.[28] This book lists the land around these three properties totalling 471 acres, 2 roods and 18 perches with an average rent/tax per acre of 71/6. The total value of the three properties is £6,546 17s 6d. John Bennett had 30 horses, 140 beast, 30 pigs, 138 sheep plus a large amount of poultry, fowl, ducks, pigeons and geese. The houses of High Field and Mount Pleasant Farms were decidedly utilitarian, with basic furnishings, and rooms for farm 'boys', and domestic 'girls'. The outdoor buildings housed carts, threshing machines, and farm implements, there were also granaries, steam houses, saddle rooms etc. With Key Field Farm, there is positive exuberance. This is after all the former home of John's mother. The house is full of mahogany furniture, and the following (*figure 42*) gives a summary of some of its contents. This must have been a supremely comfortable home. Grove House was probably even more elaborate than Key Field Farm.

On the 4th July 1885, John and Sarah Ann Bennett suffer the loss of their eldest daughter Annie Charlotte at the age of only 18. *Figure 43* shows her headstone at Whitgift Parish Church. Two months later, on 10th September, John's second son, Herbert Thomas marries at the age of 21. His wife Mary Taylor, also 21, is the daughter of John Taylor, merchant. The Taylor family lived at Bleak House in 1875. John Taylor stands for election to the Goole Local Board at the same time as John Bennett. Perhaps the two business men had this marriage lined up for some time. Herbert is already by this time a farmer in his own right. Just 10 days later, Mary Ann Sykes gives birth to her last child Mary Eleanor (registered Sykes) on 20th Sept 1885.[29]

In the space of just eleven weeks, death, marriage and birth combine to carry John on, what must have seemed like, an emotional roller coaster.

John Bennett attends Queen Victoria's Golden Jubilee in 1887, in the capacity of chairman of the Goole Local Board. According to the Royal Archives, the most likely event that he attended would be the Thanksgiving Service in Westminster Abbey on 21st June 1887.[30] The categories of guests invited to this Jubilee event included Representatives of the Chambers of Commerce and Agriculture of the United Kingdom and Ireland, and with John Bennett's involvement in this body, it is almost certain he was there.

Figure 42

No 1 bedroom:	No 2 bedroom:	No 3 bedroom:
Mahogany Tudor	Mahogany Tudor	Mahogany Tudor
Bedstead in crimson	Bedstead in crimson	Bedstead in blue rep
damask	damask	Mahogany chest
Ornaments, pictures	Various bed linen	drawers
Dressing table	Oak chest drawers	Mahogany dressing
Wash stand	2 chairs	table
Toilet service	Rocking chair	Mahogany wash stand
5 chairs	Dressing table	4 chairs
Curtains and valance	Wash stand	Plaister [sic] figure (3)
Clothes brush	Toilet service	Pictures (3)
Flower shade	Swing glass	Mantel glass rosewood
Landing:	*No 4 girls room*:	*Stair Case*
Mahogany dining table	Iron bedstead	
3 chairs	Dressing table	
Carpet	Various bed linen	
Model house		
Beer Cellar	*Store Room*	*Passage*:
		Mahogany Chiffoniere
		Mahogany hall stand
		Mahogany chairs
		Barometer
Front Kitchen:	*Pantry or Cellar*:	*Store room No 2*:
Various contents	Various contents	Various contents
Dining Room:	*Drawing room*:	
Mahogany dining table	Drawings & Pictures	
2 loose leaves	Photograph 'Ralph Creyke'	
4 mahogany chairs	4 pot dogs	
2 easy chairs	Music stool	
4 oleographs gilt	Walnut chiffoniere	
Curtains	Suite in walnut and blue rep	
Vases – lustre	Couch & 2 easy chairs	
Spittoon	6 single chairs	
Druggett	Loo table	
	Shells & ornaments	
	Medicine chest & medicine etc	

*In loving
memory of
Annie Charlotte
Bennett
Grove House
Goole
Born 25th August
1866
Died 4th July
1885*

Figure 43

In 1888, Goole sees further dock improvements with the Victoria Lock improving access for vessels. Banks Terrace has to be demolished to make way for this.

On the 11th October 1888, John's wife Sarah Ann dies. A brief announcement is made in the Goole & Marshland Weekly Times on Friday 12th October:

"At Grove House, Goole, Oct 11, Sarah Ann wife of John Bennett, aged 46 years."

*In loving
memory of
Sarah Ann
Bennett
Grove House
Goole
Born 14ᵗʰ
January 1842
Died 11ᵗʰ October
1888*

Figure 44

Sarah Ann Bennett is buried in Whitgift churchyard. The wording on her headstone (*figure 44*) is along the same lines as that of her daughter Annie Charlotte. John, apparently, nursed his wife during her illness. There is no mention of his name, however, on her headstone. John would now be free to marry Mary Ann Sykes and set up one home for their combined families. He leaves a respectable (but short) period of just under three months before they marry on the 2nd January 1889 at St.Peter's Church in Brighton (*figure 45*). Perhaps for them this is a symbolic 'new start' at the start of the New Year. Maybe they spent Christmas with their children, and then left for the fashionable Victorian town of

Brighton. Brighton may have been a favourite place for them, or perhaps it was just a spur of the moment decision to marry there. The decision to marry well away from home was perhaps an attempt to keep the wedding as low key as possible. The couple by doing this could avoid the possibility of upsetting John's children by Sarah Ann. There is no evidence to show that any of them attended. John and Mary Ann marry by licence in the presence of Mary (or Mrs) Robinson and Mary Ann's sister Emily Eleanor Sykes. John and Mary Ann's residence given on the marriage certificate is "The Grand Hotel, Brighton". An opulent choice of hotel, and maybe they had booked a few nights for the New Year celebration and marriage. John was 52 years of age and Mary Ann 45. The Grand, built in 1864, was still relatively 'new' in building terms. St Peter's Church, built between 1824 and 1828, designed by Charles Barry (later to be the architect of the Houses of Parliament) became the parish church of Brighton in 1873. *Figure 46*, a photograph of the Grand Hotel taken around 1880, shows how it would have looked when John and Mary Ann stayed there for their marriage. Mary Ann had been a widow for twenty years, and it had been eighteen years since she and John had their first child together. Their youngest daughter Mary Eleanor was just 3 years old at the time her parents married. Mary Ann lived with her children at 9 South Parade, Doncaster right up to this time, as seen from Kelly's Directory of 1889.

Back home, just a few days later, a tragic incident involving the India is reported in this short newspaper article in the Goole Weekly Times Friday 11th January 1889:

"A GOOLE SAILOR DROWNED AT BLACKTOFT – Yesterday morning Robert Kendal, sailor on board the s.s. India, which left Goole some hours previously, was drowned whilst the steamer was lying alongside Blacktoft jetty. The deceased who was a young man recently married, resided in Milson Terrace."

Figure 45

Like John, this young man had recently married. John, with the happiness of his own wedding just a few days past, must have felt deeply for the sailor's young widow.

John Bennett's Red Cross Line is developing extremely well and he is operating a regular service with his vessels. Major changes, however, are on the horizon. Albert Chatelle writes of the company:

"It was to profit more over from a commercial incident, which, towards 1889 was provoking serious thought in the maritime circles of Boulogne especially amongst Forwarding Agents and Commission Brokers". The trigger for this change occurs at the end of 1889, when the General Steam Navigation Company announces that it is cancelling its service with Boulogne. Albert Chatelle continues the story "thanks to the spirit of initiative of the two Boulogne Notables – Etienna Carmier and Longuety, two steamers had been chartered by them from 1889 to run a shuttle between Boulogne and London. A letter in the local press in January

69

1890 at the instance of M. Jules Petit, one of the active Forwarding Agents, summarised trenchantly the situation – It is a question, he said, of conserving for our port an important and coveted traffic."

Figure 46

An attempt made to establish the Boulogne Steamship Company encountered certain difficulties. John Bennett, who is already making three sailings per week from Boulogne to Goole on Mondays, Wednesdays and Fridays, decides to fill the void created by the departure of the General Steam Navigation Company. In order to fund this new venture, he needed to raise capital by transforming his Red Cross Line into a limited company that would float on the stock exchange. A new chapter in the company is about to begin.

Kelly's Directory of the West Riding of Yorkshire shows the chief shipping companies in the town of Goole, in 1889:

"The Goole Steam Shipping Company Limited have a fleet of eight large first-class screw steamers for the Continental trade and passengers; Mr. John Bennett has three powerful screw steamers in the Boulogne trade; the Humber Steam Shipping Company Limited have three first-class screw steamers engaged in the Ghent and Jersey trade; the Yorkshire Coal and Steam Ship Company Limited have five powerful screw steamers in the Hamburg and Rouen trade; Mr William France Limited has seven powerful screw steamers in the Goole and London trade; the Co-operative Wholesale Society have four powerful steamers in the Hamburg and Calais trade; there are also the Goole and Hull Steam Packet Company Limited, for daily passenger traffic, and the Goole and Hull Steam Towing Company Limited have eight steam tugs which find ample employment."

It is not difficult to imagine the need for expansion of the Goole Docks to cope with all this marine traffic.

Chapter 5
Time for Expansion

In 1890, John Bennett purchases the Berlin for his own fleet, as announced in The Goole Weekly Times, Friday 4th April 1890. A transcription of the notice can be seen in *figure 47*.

"The s.s. Berlin, which, since 1879, has been running between Goole and Hamburg, has been sold by the Yorkshire Coal and Steam Ship Company, Limited, to Mr John Bennett, who has purchased her with the intention of including her in the Red Cross Line of steamers running between Goole and Boulogne.

Figure 47

He renames this ship the 'Malta' in true Bennett style, and a photograph can be seen in *figure 49*. John Bennett takes a significant step to transform his business, as reported in the same edition of the newspaper. A transcription of the notice can be seen in *figure 48*.

"Friday, April 4th, 1890
NEW LIMITED COMPANY FOR GOOLE – We hear that Mr John Bennett, steam ship-owner, of Goole, and Boulogne-sur-Mer has converted his business into a limited company, the registered capital being £100,000 divided into 10,000 shares of £10 each. The first issue is one of £60,000. We believe there has already been a large number of shares allotted to French shippers and merchants, and that a portion of the remainder is reserved, but will be offered privately to English manufacturers and shippers."

Figure 48

Figure 49

Figure 50

73

Perhaps the plan to expand his fleet coincides with the expansion of the business. John Bennett installs himself in London, whilst his elder son John manages the Goole operation. Another of his sons, Robert Bennett, related earlier in this story on board ship bound for Boulogne, is managing the Boulogne operation. At this time, the Boulogne office relocates from Quai Bonaparte to Quai Chanzy. Departures for London take place from Boulogne at 7pm on Tuesdays, Thursdays, and Saturdays. Departures for Goole and Hull are on Mondays, Wednesdays and Saturdays at the same hour. The Bennett family is assisted in London by Mr Connor and in Boulogne by Monsieur Bertholoot. The Adam Bank, founded in 1784, loaned the company money during this time of expansion. This bank had a branch at 6 Rue Victor Hugo, Boulogne, the same street in which the Bennett company had their office. The postcard (*figure 50*) shows an advertisement for the bank on the end of this building between Quai Gambetta and Rue de Boston. John Bennett and members of his family hold many of the shares in the new company, and the scope of the business has now been widened by the acquisition of a steamer service between London and Boulogne. John Bennett has by this time become a Justice of the Peace, and references to him in the local newspapers use the initials "J.P." after his name.

In the previous week the newspapers were reporting on the Coal Strike, and in particular how it was affecting the port of Goole. The Goole Weekly Times, Friday 28th March 1890, reports as follows:

"The Goole Steam Shipping Company having had a good supply of bunker coal – as appears to have been the case with the whole of the ship owners in the port – were enabled to run their steamers as ordinarily." It continues, "the Hydra steamer, belonging to Mr John Bennett, has been laid up in consequence of the strike, and so also has the Berlin, belonging to the Yorkshire Coal and Steam Ship Company".

John Bennett did not allow the Coal Strike to interfere with his expansion plans, and negotiations to purchase the Berlin must already have been well under way. The Shipping List, in The Goole Weekly Times on Friday 4th April 1890, shows the China bringing in goods from Boulogne, the Hydra (now sailing again) and the India are both bringing in goods from Ghent, Belgium.

John now decides to sell 9 South Parade, Doncaster, as he obviously has no further use for it. On 9th April 1890, the deed to this property transfers from John, to James Batty, 'Gent' of Doncaster.[31] John used a solicitor from Doncaster when he first purchased this property, this time, however, his witness is William Frank, Commercial Clerk of Goole. The deed stated that this property was previously in the occupation of John Bennett and made no mention of occupation by Mary Ann possibly to keep this chapter of his life veiled in secrecy.

At the end of April in the same year, John Bennett is one of the donors towards the cost of building the new Primitive Methodist Chapel at Garthorpe. He donates £10 to the fund. A stone-laying ceremony and public tea accompanies the laying of the foundation stone.

The following photograph (*figure 51*) shows children from both of John Bennetts' families on a garden bench, possibly at Grove House. The estimated date of this photograph is between 1888 and 1890.

On 27th August 1890, John Bennett transfers his deed to 3702 square yards of land in Old Goole close to his home, to William Everatt Hind of Goole.[32] It is difficult to ascertain exactly which piece of land this transaction covers. A couple of months later on the 27th October, John transfers a small portion of land to Richard Fosdick, merchant of Rawcliffe.[33] This land comprises 147 square yards between the newly made

Figure 51

Back row from left: Albert Edmund (Hal), Arthur Frederick,
Front row from left: Mary Adelaide (Polly), Sarah Ann (Sallie),
Mary Eleanor (Mopsy), Edith Elizabeth (Tiddy)

"H T BENNETT
SWINEFLEET
WILL in future act as AGENT for Mr. T. Wilkinson,
Corn Merchant, Barnsley, for the Goole and
Marshland District."

Figure 52

Stanhope Street and Mariners Street, with messuages or dwelling houses on it.

Another serious incident occurs in the town of Goole on Wednesday 28th January 1891, when a fire breaks out at the Market Hall in Goole. The Goole Weekly Times reports this on Friday 30th January 1891:

"The whole of the property belonging to the Goole Market Hall Company Limited, with the exception of the armoury and one adjoining shop, were destroyed by fire". It goes on to account "Mr Watson, in the employ of the Humber Steam Shipping Company, succeeded in ascending the staircase to the first floor, and rescuing from the office of the company a book of considerable value." Ten pianofortes were lost, along with offices and goods belonging to several local businesses. The article goes on "From enquiries we made we learn that the Market Hall Company are insured in the Alliance Insurance Company for £5000". Other businesses were not insured.

At the time of the 1891 census, on the evening of the 5th April the only family members at Grove House are, Arthur Frederick, his half sister Mary (Adelaide) and sister Isabel (*see figure 55*). Perhaps the two servants (born at Doncaster) came with Mary Ann and her family when she married John Bennett and moved to Grove House. John Bennett junior, married to Elizabeth, lives at 19 Heber Terrace (*see figure 56*). Herbert Thomas, married to Mary Taylor, lives at Keyfield House, his grandmother's former home (*see figure 57*). They have two sons, Stanley aged 4 and Herbert aged 2. Also in the household are two of Herbert and Mary's nieces, and a staff of nine. Herbert Thomas is himself now an agent for a Corn Merchant and is advertising this fact in the local press. *Figure 52* shows a transcription of this advertisement from The Goole Weekly Times newspaper, Friday 16th January 1891.

On census night, John and Mary Ann Bennett are staying at the Victoria Hotel in North Meols, Southport. With them, is their son John aged 10, and daughter Mary Eleanor aged 7. Staying in the Hotel are various merchants, a captain in the army, and numerous others. Whether John and Mary Ann are simply on a short break or this is a business trip, cannot be determined. There was a strong connection with Southport, shown earlier in the story, as many of their children were born in this area. Southport was the third largest seaside resort in the country in the 1880s. The Victoria Hotel opened in 1842, and many wealthy and noble families stayed there (*figure 53*). Their daughter, Edith Elizabeth, aged 15, was on census day, at a school in Harrogate named 'Ashbourne'. The school Principal was Ann Brewer, widow aged 72. This is following the pattern of her older half-sisters ten years earlier. Later in this chapter some aspects of school life for Edith will be seen through her diary of the following year. Found in the census also is an Albert E Bennett aged 18, a private with the regiment of the Argyll and Sutherland Highlanders. He gave his birth county as Middlesex, but his birth parish unknown. This is possibly John and the late Sarah Ann's son. Most of their children were baptised at St. Bartholomew's church, Eastoft, but there is no evidence of an Albert Edmund baptised there. It is possible, therefore, that his birth and baptism take place in Middlesex for some reason. Edith Elizabeth records in her diary, that Albert 'crossed the line' (the equator) in September 1892. It is possible that he was being moved with his regiment to a theatre of war in the British Empire at that time.

The newly formed Bennett Steamship Company Limited is now advertising its steamers and time table (see *figure* 54) in The Goole Weekly Times Friday 17th April 1891.

Figure 53

Figure 54

Figure 55 - Census 1891 – Goole

| Abode | Person | Relationship To Head Of Family | Cond* | Age | | Rank, Profession Or Occupation | Where Born |
				Male	Female		
Grove House, Marshland Road, Goole	Arthur Bennett	Son		19		Sea Marine Engineer app.	Doncaster
	Mary Bennett	Dau			22		Adlingfleet
	Isabel Bennett	Dau			17		Lytham, Lancs
	Alice Melling	Serv			19	Domestic Servant Cook	Doncaster
	Emily Day	Serv			18	Domestic Servant Housemaid	Doncaster

*Condition

Figure 56 - Census 1891 – Goole

Abode	Person	Relationship To Head Of Family	Cond*	Age		Rank, Profession Or Occupation	Where Born
				Male	Female		
Heber Terrace, Goole	John Bennett jnr	Head	M	29		Manager Bennett SS Co Ltd	Adlingfleet, Yorks
	Elizabeth Bennett	Wife	M		26		Goole, Yorks
	Charlotte Lister	Serv	S		19	General Domestic Servant	Thorne, Yorks

*Condition   M=Married   S=Single

Figure 57 - Census 1891 - Swinefleet & Reedness (following image)

Abode	Person	Relation To Head	Cond*	Age		Rank, Prof. Or Occ.	Where Born
				Male	Female		
Keyfield House,	Herbert Thos Bennett	Head	M	27		Farmer	Yorks, Sandhill
	Mary Bennett	Wife	M		27		Lancs, Liverpool
	Stanley	Son		4			Yorks, Swinefleet
	Herbert M Bennett	Son		2			Yorks, Swinefleet
	Dora K Armitage	Niece			9	Scholar	Yorks, Goole
	Elsie M Armitage	Niece			5		Yorks, Goole
	Kate Everatt	Serv	S		22	Dom.Servant	Lincs, Eastoft
	Alice Emerson	Serv	S		17	Dom.Servant	Lincs, Eastoft
	Jane Farr	Nurse	Wid		68	Dom.Servant	Norfolk, K Lynn
	Albert Brown	Serv	S			Farm Servant	Yorks, Eastoft
	Charlie Dilcott	Groom	S	19		Groom Dom.	Yorks, Laxton
	Alfred Bivinn	Serv	S	18		Farm Servant	Lincs, Eastoft
	Henry Torn	Serv	S	17		Farm Servant	Yorks, Ousefleet
	Frederick Lawson	Serv	S	16		Farm Servant	Yorks, Swinefleet
	Elmer Arrand	Serv	S	14		Farm Servant	Lincs, Belton

*Condition   M=Married   S=Single   Wid=Widow

Figure 58

Figure 59

The two photographs (*figures 58 and 59*) show Bennett ships in the docks at Goole. *Figure 58* shows the Africa, a vessel yet to come into the company being loaded with locomotives. *Figure 59* shows various steamships alongside sailing vessels.

H. Lormier   Boulogne-sur-Mer

Figure 60

This photograph (*figure 60*) appears to be one of the captains (identity unknown) of the Bennett Company, taken by a photographer in Boulogne - A Lormier. He has the Red Cross emblem on the badge on his hat.

The previous company advertisement shows that John has established an office at 'Quai Chauzy' (now referred to as Chanzy), Boulogne-sur-Mer, and at 29 Tooley Street, London. The company is now growing at a steady pace. The growth in the shipping trade can also be seen at this time.

Albert Chatelle recounts that, for 1891, there was considerable growth in the amount of cargo passing through Boulogne compared with 1881. In 1891, the port moves "9,410,000 cases fruit, 5,242,000 kgs vegetables and 7,808,000 kgs potatoes."

In the summer of the same year, John Bennett purchases yet another vessel, the ss Burma. The Selby Express announces this on Friday 10th July 1891:

"On Saturday last the new steamer Burma, constructed by Messrs S.P.Austin and Son, of the Wear Dock yard, for the

Bennett Steamship Company, Limited, of Goole, was taken out on trial. After the compasses were adjusted, the vessel proceeded to Whitley for the purpose of trying her speed on the measured mile off that place and the weather being favourable, a series of progressive speed trials were gone through, giving results ranging from 20 to 96 revolutions per minute, with speed from 12 to 13.5 knots per hour. These results were considered to be highly satisfactory, and, after the friends had been landed at Sunderland, the steamer proceeded on her voyage to Goole, from which port she is intended to trade to the French Channel, in connection with the line already established by the company. The vessel has been constructed under Lloyd's special survey for the transport of light and perishable goods, and designed to attain a high speed, and to enter ports at a shallow draft. The engines have been constructed by Messrs George Clark, Southwick Engine Works. The company on board during the trial included the managing director of the company, Mr John Bennett, the manager Mr. J. Bennett, jun., Capt. Armytage, Mr. H.T. Bennett, Mr. A. Bennett, and other friends of the company, Mr Selwyn Austin and Mr R. Macoll representing the builders of the vessel, and Mr. Geo. Clark representing the makers of the machinery. The senior captain of the company, Capt.Ingleby, will take command of the new vessel."

Why John changed shipbuilder from W B Thompson (who had built the last ship), to this one is not clear. The Burma's gross tonnage is 724, and her registered ship number is 98382. *Figure 61* shows a photograph of the Burma, and her specification can be seen in *figure 62*. The shipping list, in The Goole Weekly Times Friday 24th July 1891, shows the first arrival of the Burma on the 23rd July under the command of Captain Ingleby, with a cargo of 'goods'. As mentioned in the article on the Burma, Captain Ingleby is the senior captain for the company, and it seems that he has the privilege of taking the helm of each new vessel that comes into the fleet.

Figure 61

Figure 62

Ship No	98382
Name	Burma
Description	Steel Screw Schooner
Master	J Ingleby – 76-91
Tonnage	Gross 724, Under deck 536, net 264
Dimensions	Length – 203.3 Breadth – 30.1 Depth – 13.5
Engines	T.3Cy.19", 30" & 49"-33" 160lb 120 HP by G Clark Ltd Sunderland
Builder	S P Austin & Son, Sunderland
Built	1891 7mo
Owner	Bennett Steam Ship Co Ltd
Registered port	Goole
Port of survey	Sunderland
Class	100 A1 (built under special survey)

Captain Foster now commands the China; Captain Colbridge commands the Malta. At the same time as the purchase of this new vessel the Burma, the railway dock in Goole is undergoing extension. Perhaps this necessity is due to the growth in the fleet of the Bennett Steamship Company, and other companies using the port. An artist impression of the extended dock can be seen in The Goole Weekly Times on Friday 31st July. *Figure 63* gives a transcription of the caption underneath this illustration. The shipping list, for one week in September 1891, shows the increased amount of marine traffic. In just three days, there were 48 vessels arriving at, and sailing from, the port of Goole. It must have been a hive of activity and the main source of employment in the town.

> *"The above gives a view of the new dock as it appeared while the water was flowing into it. The dimensions of the dock are about four acres, it being 620 feet long, 260 feet broad, and 22 feet deep. When completed the coffer dam at the far end will be entirely removed, and there will be one large sheet of water from the quay close to the Lancashire and Yorkshire South Sheds to Stanhope Street."*

Figure 63

The town of Goole was growing rapidly in other ways. 1891 sees the construction and opening of the Post Office situated at the corner of North Street and Victoria Street, and the Arcade that connected the same two streets further along. The arcade contained sixteen shops and still exists with its Victorian iron and glass domed roof. The total cost at the time was £10,000. Also at the beginning of this year, the Cottage Hospital, presented to the town by W H Bartholomew Esquire of Leeds, opened on Boothferry Road. It later became known as the Bartholomew Hospital and only closed in the late 20th century.

On the 24th September 1891, the China is involved in a collision, on the River Humber. A brief account of the incident appears in The Goole Weekly Times the following day:

"COLLISION IN THE HUMBER – Yesterday morning, while the ss China, of Goole, was lying at anchor in Hull Roads, a German steamer collided with her, doing considerable damage to her stem plates. The China has put into Hull for repairs."

So temporarily, the company fleet reduces to four vessels again. Whereas the company has previously operated from offices at Railway Dock Goole, they are about to go upmarket into new premises called the 'New Bank Buildings' (later renamed 'Bank Chambers') on the corner of Stanhope Street and Church Street. This pretty impressive building, designed by Mr H B Thorp, architect of Goole, is today used as Council offices. The building, commissioned by Beckett & Company's Bank, cost £20,000. Most of the main shipping companies re-located to this grand property. The Goole Weekly Times of Friday 4th December 1891 gives a full description and illustration of the "New Bank Buildings" (*figure 64*). In the following excerpt from this article, the extent of the Bennett Steamship Company occupation can be seen:

"The ground floor in Stanhope Street has already been rented by the Bennett Steamship Company, Limited, and Mr. T.L. Williams. The Bennett Steamship Company's suite consists of a clerk's room, 44 feet long by 19 feet wide; two manager's and book-keepers offices, 20 feet 6 inches by 15 feet; and a private office, 15 feet by 15 feet."

The building has hardly changed today, as seen from the picture taken in 2003 (*figure 65*). Only in recent years has the Bennett Steam Ship Company sign been removed. I remember this imposing building as a young child, and reading the Bennett sign every time I passed it. It was, and still is, a major landmark in Goole.

THE GOOLE WEEKLY TIMES

THE NEW BANK BUILDINGS AT GOOLE.

NEW BANK AND SUITES OF OFFICES, GOOLE, FOR MESSRS BECKETT AND COMPANY & HENRY BELL THORP, ARCHITECT, GOOLE.

DESCRIPTIVE SKETCH.

One of the most noticeable features in connection with the growth of Goole has been the numerous handsome structures that have been erected in the town during the last year or two. But undoubtedly the most important from an architectural point of view is the splendid block now in course of construction—and, by the way, rapidly approaching completion—at the corner of Church and Stanhope streets. These premises, which are commonly known as the "New Bank Buildings," are being erected for Messrs Beckett & Co., the well-known Leeds bankers, and are destined to take the place of the unpretentious offices in Boothferry-road, Goole, in which they have carried on their business since they opened a branch in this town. The architect of the new building is Mr H. B. Thorp, of Goole, who may be congratulated on the elegance of the structure he has designed. It forms one of the finest suites of offices in Yorkshire, in addition to the fact that it will be the finest building of which Goole can at present boast. It fronts Stanhope-street and Church-street, its length in the former street being 105 feet, and in the latter 105 feet. The building is freely treated in the renaissance style, to be adapted to the purpose for which it is required, and is faced with Ruabon bricks and red terra cotta dressings throughout, from Mr J. C. Edwards, Ruabon. The façade has a most imposing appearance. At the angle at the meeting of the two streets is the bank entrance, with a semi-circular arch, carried on fluted pilasters, with panelled soffit. This angle is further enriched by oriel windows, and a terra cotta turret. The bank premises are at the corner of the two streets, and consist of a handsome banking room, the walls and ceilings of which will be finished in fibrous plaster mouldings and panels; the floors will be of red tiles, and the desks, screens, &c., of polished Honduras mahogany, to the designs furnished by the architect. There is in the rear a strong room lined with glazed bricks, with Price's strong room door and grill, and the walls are of great

thickness, while the floor is of concrete. Accommodation is provided in each street for two large blocks of offices. The ground floor in Stanhope-street has already been rented by the Bennett Steamship Company, Limited, and Mr T. Ll. Williams. The Bennett Steamship Company's suite consists of a clerks' room, 44 feet long by 19 feet wide; two managers' and book-keeper's offices, 20 feet 6 inches by 15 feet; and a private office, 15 feet by 15 feet. The whole of the first floor in Stanhope-street is taken up by Mr A. Mack and the Yorkshire Coal and Steamship Company. It comprises a clerks' office, 44 feet by 19 feet; book-keeper's and manager's office, 20 feet by 15 feet; two private offices, 15 feet by 15 feet; a directors' room, 25 feet by 15 feet; a captain's waiting room, 19 feet by 16 feet; and a strong room—the whole forming a capital set of offices. On the ground floor in Church-street offices are rented by Messrs England & Son, solicitors, Goole; they consist of five rooms 16 feet square, and a strong room. There is a further set of four offices on the first floor, and similar offices to these below on the second floor in both Church and Stanhope streets. The private entrance to the bank manager's house is in Church-street, and his apartments comprise commodious sitting rooms, kitchens, &c., on the first floor, and on the second floor there are six bed rooms, bath room, &c. All the different sets of offices have private lavatories, &c., which are lined with glazed bricks, and fitted up with the latest sanitary improvements. It is proposed to light the building with gas at present, but wires are being laid throughout; the whole of the rooms, with the idea of using electricity should it be adopted by the town. The total cost of the building will be about £10,000. The contractors for the work are Messrs W. Nicholson and Son, of Leeds, who are to be congratulated on the excellency of their workmanship, and the following are the sub-contractors:—Slating, Mr Season, Leeds; plumbing, Mr J. Lindley, Leeds; painting, Mr Barron, Goole; plastering, Mr Mountain, Leeds; terra cotta work, Mr J. C. Edwards, Ruabon; lightning conductors, Messrs Berry and Son, Huddersfield.

Figure 64

89

At that time I did not know of the family connections. This picture shows only the frontage to Stanhope Street. The building stretches almost the same distance along Church Street.

Figure 65

What an eventful year 1891 turned out to be for the town of Goole and the company.

Figure 66 is an advertisement from The Goole Weekly Times newspaper on the 1st January 1892, showing the full Bennett fleet. At the beginning of 1892, John Bennett chaired a meeting of the winding up of the Goole Market Hall Company. The meeting sees John appointed as liquidator for the company on behalf of the shareholders. The Goole Weekly Times, Friday 8th January 1892, reports:

"the CHAIRMAN said that before the resolution was put to the meeting he wished to say that as regards the costs of the liquidator he would want nothing himself, but he proposed to ask Mr Haldenby to act as his clerk, who he thought should be paid some reasonable amount for his services". It goes on "Mr BLOW proposed, and Captain ROBINSON seconded a vote of thanks to Mr Bennett, which was adopted". John Bennett continued "The company had done its best to provide market accommodation at a time when there was no suitable place in Goole, but the time had come when it had fallen to the lot of some other body to make the provision".

Figure 66

John Bennett decides that after carrying out his role as liquidator, he will no longer be involved in the new company. Perhaps the shipping business and his role as Justice of the Peace are now his 'business' priorities.

John and Mary Ann's daughter Edith Elizabeth kept a diary, as was common practice until more recent times. Her diary for 1892 still exists and offers a glimpse of, and some insight into, the family routines during this time. Edith, like her older half sisters, also attended private school in Harrogate as seen in the 1891 Census. Towards the end of January, she is returning to school as documented in her diary.

"27 January Finished packing. Came to school. Belle, Sally, Jack and Mary see me off."

Belle is her older sister Isabel; Sally is her older half sister, Sarah Ann; Jack her younger brother baptised John; Mary the youngest of the family of John and Mary Ann Bennett.

At the other side of the English Channel, the Bennett Steamship Company has offices at 'Quai Chauzy' as previously mentioned. An old photograph (*figure 67*) shows the port of Boulogne. Although the exact date of this photograph is unknown, the presence of sailing ships in the foreground demonstrates that it must be fairly early. Several funnels of steam ships can be seen around the quayside, and one particularly half way along the far side of the quay, does seem to have the cross of the Bennett Steamship Company on a white background. As previously mentioned, the company at this time is also trading from a London office at 29 Tooley Street close to London Bridge. This story will go on to tell of new offices eventually built at 15 Tooley Street.

Figure 67

Back at her school in Harrogate, Edith's diary continues.

"10 February Lesson in morning. Walk over Harlow Moor. Drilling in the afternoon. Dancing in the evening."

92

Figure 68

The photograph *figure 68* shows the appearance of the moor even though this image is some years later circa 1909. The diary continues.

"*12 February Lessons with Mademoiselle in the afternoon. Walk over Harlow Hill in the evening.*"

"*13 February Write letter. Went for ride. Went out with Mrs Brown and Kathleen to café afternoon*".

In the 1891 census return mentioned earlier in the chapter, a Kathleen Brown aged 14 of Tynemouth, Northumberland appears at Ashbourne school. This is clearly the Kathleen mentioned above, with Mrs Brown assumed to be her mother.

"*15 February Got up 7.30. Breakfast, lessons, drawing, stop in at 12 and read, dinner, read after dinner, lessons until 4.30. Go in the town with Miss Auburn. Tea. After tea read. Mr Spinks lecture on Australia.*"

The 1891 census records Miss Auburn as the Teacher of

English at the school. Mr Spinks may well be the father of Ingham Spinks, who Edith would later go on to marry. In fact, the census records a Louisa May Spink, scholar; possibly Mr Spinks is her father, and indeed Edith later mentions 'May' Spinks.

Edith studied French, as no doubt so had her sisters before her. This was the fashion of the time for young educated ladies and would also have had a practical advantage for the Bennett family with their connections over in France. Sister Isabel and half sister Mary Adelaide (Polly) visit Edith at the beginning of March.

"2 March Ash Wednesday Go to the station to meet Belle and Polly. Go to café. Have dinner with Polly and Belle. Kathleen and I go in town to café."

On the 13th April, presumably for Easter, Edith leaves for home.

"13 April Breakfasted and went to Leeds 9.6 [train] *arrived home 12. Belle, Polly and Mary met us* [Edith and her friend Kathleen] *with carriage. Had dinner and played in garden, tea and then to bed."*

A delightful, long Easter break for Edith, she returns a month later.

"14 May Sat in the garden in the morning. Went for a drive with Mother. Came back to school arrived in Harrogate 7.30."

On the 6th June her parents and youngest sister visit.

"6 June Mother, Father and Mary came to see me, had dinner at the Prospect, went for a drive, had tea. Went to Birk Crag in the evening."

Figure 69

Figure 70

Figure 69 is a view looking south from Prospect Square, to the Prospect Hotel, circa 1890. *Figure 70* shows a photograph of Birk Crag taken circa 1908, sixteen years after Edith's diary entry.

Then home again 30th June – Edith's birthday.

"30 June Went home in the evening arrived 8, supper, bed"

The next day Edith is playing tennis at Grove House, and the family enjoying the use of a tent they have in the garden. The photograph (seen earlier in the chapter) of John's children on a garden bench appears to be taken just before the year of this diary; Edith seated on the far right. She returns to school on the 4th July.

"4 July   Read in the morning.   Dinner.   Sat in the tent and talked to Mother, Polly, Sally and Belle – came to school by 4.30"

A week later Edith is taking her exams – Geography 11th July, History on the 13th, Arithmetic the 18th, French on the 20th, and Old Testament exam 22nd July. Exams over, Edith sets out for home again.

"28 July   Got up and finished packing.   Went home by 9 train.   When I got home Mrs Carr was there.   Had dinner. After dinner sat in the tent.   Played cricket in the afternoon."

Mrs Carr may have been the wife of the Reverend Carr, Vicar of Goole. Some members of the Bennett family go over to Boulogne for a summer holiday. Over the following weeks in her diary, Edith records this trip. They most likely sailed on one of the Bennett company vessels and certainly returned on the Burma.

"4 August   Packed and fussed etc.   Had dinner.   "Higgle piggled".   Next to the station.   I met Father.   Came back

home. *Went with Sarai* [Sally] *to the boat. Started on our voyage about 3 o'clock. Had tea just out of Hull Roads. Went to bed."*

Hull Roads is an area in the River Humber close to the present Alexandria Dock.

"5 August   Got up had breakfast. Arrived at Boulogne about 2.30. Low water so Bob came with a "ficht[?] Bateau" and took us ashore. No [unclear] *on the sands until 8, had tea aboard and went to* [unclear] *in the evening – slept with Sally that night."*

Bob is Robert, Edith's older half brother, based over in Boulogne looking after the French side of the company.

"6 August   Went in the town with the Pater [Father] *got bathing costumes, bathed – had dinner and went to the Sailors Institute to get some books."*

"Sunday 7 August   Went on the sands in the morning, read in the afternoon – Church in the afternoon."

"8 August   Bathed in the morning. Captain Armitage came to dinner. Read in the afternoon and evening."

This is possibly Captain Godfrey Armitage J.P. who attended her father's funeral in 1904.

"9 August   So excited on my tale that I began reading at 6 in the morning and read until dinner. Bob came. Went to the library with Mother and Sally, then on the sands and to the fair with Belle and Sally."

"10 August   Bathed in the morning and went with Jacques [Jack] *for a row, then to Cavengs* [place unidentified]."*

"*11 August   Bathed in the morning, had dinner and went on the sands.   In the evening I went to the fair with Belle and Sally.*"

"*12 August   Went on the sands.   Belle read us a tale. Bathed. Bob came. Played cricket in the afternoon. Went with Jacques to the fair to get birds.*"

"*13 August   Sad tale.   Mary let one of my birds out. Bathed. Went to the market with Mother. Went to the fair with Mother, Jack and May. Went in the town with Jack to Cavengs. Rained fast.*"

"*Sunday 14 August Went to Church in the morning. Read in the afternoon and evening. Finished "Olive".*"

"*15 August   Sat on the sands in the morning. Bathed in the afternoon.   Went with Sally and Belle to the fair in the evening.*"

"*16 August   Sat on the sands.   Bathed in the afternoon. Went to the fair with Sally and Belle.*"

"*17 August   Bathed in the morning played cricket in the afternoon. Went to the circus Rancy.*"

"*18 August   Got up three o'clock. Went to the boat [Boulogne], got aboard about 4.30. Reached Folkestone about 7.10, landed and had breakfast. Went all over Folkestone. Went to Dover by train 12.13. On the beach, had tea and then went back to Folkestone by train – rained fast – rushed to the boat, got aboard wet through. Sailed, lightning (fork) all the way home. Arrived at Boulogne 10.20. Had supper, got to bed 12pm.*"

"*19 August   Bathed. Tried to put up the tent. Roy, Enid and Paddy came to tea.*"

"20 August   Bathed – read in the morning.   Went to Cavengs in the town"

"Sunday 21 August Read in the morning. Went for a drive to see procession. Church in the evening."

"22 August   Went on the sands. Had drive in the afternoon. Went for row in the evening."

"23 August   Went on the sands and read. Sat on the sands in the afternoon   Went in the town with Mother."

"24 August   Elsie's birthday. Packed. Went in town. Went to the centre and museum in the afternoon. Tea. Played cards. Go aboard Burma."

"25 August   Had tea in the bunk. Got up and went on deck then to sleep. Felt rather bad (seasick). Dinner. Got to Hull about 4.20. Came to Goole by train."

On Sarah Ann's birthday, 2nd September, the family celebrates in the following way.

"2 September Sally's birthday.   Had tennis party.   Mr Herring, Mr Gilbert, Mr Seine King, Nellie and Joe Bunker came to tea. Played games in the evening."

Two weeks later, the family gives even more elaborate celebrations in the form of a ball.

"15 September Came home. Kathleen came to Newcastle with me. Arrive Goole about 3 o'clock. Had dinner and helped get things ready for ball."

"16 September Arthur went in the town – after dinner helped to decorate "Elbie".   Ball in the evening.   Enjoyed it immensely. Bed five am"

This was quite a late night for a 16 year old. Edith also records a key moment for her half brother when he crosses the equator on the 24th September.

"24 September Albert crossed the line and met a barque called the "Aires" bound to call west coast of America 24 days out."

John Bennett and his wife Mary Ann travel to London on the 14th November. It is Mary Ann's birthday the following day, so perhaps this is a birthday treat. Mary Ann returns home on the 19th November; presumably her husband stays in London.

Finally for 1892 Christmas Day as documented by Edith.

"On Christmas Day I got up pretty early and looked at the presents I had got from Belle, Polly and Sally. After breakfast, we all went to church. When we came in it was nearly time for dinner. John, Mrs John and Elsie came to dinner and Mr Todd was also there. We had a jolly dinner. Afterwards we went in the library and I played tiddleywinks with Belle, John and Sally. Later on I nursed Elsie a little after Arthur read us a tale. Then we had tea. After tea we talked a little round the dining room fire. Mrs Herbert and Stanley came in to afternoon tea."

Edith records in her diary, details of her pocket money for the year - *see table right*. She has also written in the back an address in Boulogne – 74, Boulevard de Ste Beuve. The relevance of this address is unknown. It may have been somewhere she stayed when the family visited or, just a hotel address.

Father	£	12	13	9
Mother	£	3	15	0
John	£		4	6
Total	£	16	13	3

The postcard *(figure 71)* shows this street (exact date unknown).

21. *BOULOGNE-SUR-MER. — Perspective du Boulevard Sainte-Beuve. — LL.*

Figure 71

The 8th September 1893 sees John Bennett appointed as one of the unofficial Trustees of the Hook and Goole Charity.[34]

More of John Bennett's older children are now marrying and having families of their own. In 1894, the family have a double celebration when both Mary Adelaide and Sarah Ann marry on the 1st August in a double wedding. Mary Adelaide marries Daniel Hewitt Todd (native of Hull) an engineer, and Sarah Ann marries her cousin Walter Brunyee of Eastoft farmer (sixth son of Ann Brunyee nee Bennett, John's sister). On the marriage certificate, the residence given for Daniel Hewitt Todd is Grove House, Old Goole; he is obviously living with the Bennett family at the time of the wedding. The witnesses for Mary and Daniel are J Herring and Belle (Isabel) Bennett. The officiating minister is Jas. H Fry M.A. Chaplain of Boulogne. Sarah and Walter's witnesses are George Major and Rosa Kate Brunyee (Walter's sister). The minister is William H Carr. What a joyous occasion this must have been for the families concerned. The Anglo-French connection is abundantly clear with the ministers chosen.

Later that month on the 28th August an incident occurs in the docks at Goole which must have caused quite a stir, and indeed affects the operations into and out of the port. 150 'Tom Puddings', fully loaded with 35-40 tons of coal each, lie chained together in Germany dock ready to be towed the following morning. Tom Puddings were iron compartment boats fastened together in a long 'train' to be pulled along the canal by steamboats from the collieries in the West Riding. The dock operatives suspected that, in the early hours of the morning, one of the 'boats' appears to have filled with water by means of a leak and sunk. The disastrous result of this initial sinking drags the remaining attached boats to the bottom one after the other; nearly 70 sank. The Daily News of the 30th August 1894 [35] referring to the accident states:

"The folly of putting all your eggs into one basket is proverbial; but what should be said of the man who, having put his eggs into many baskets, fastens them together, so that the downfall of one must bring all the others to destruction?"

What a stir and disruption this must have caused in the town; the audience on the quayside watching the slow process of retrieval.

The year 1895 arrived with the rumours around the town of Goole of a possible amalgamation between three of the large shipping companies. Many in the town perceived this as a detrimental step, with the only people to gain being the capitalists, and those most affected being the workers whose employment may be at risk. It was of concern to the dock labourers, agents, and clerks, as indeed the managers that such concentration of business would result in a corresponding reduction of managers, and a general reduction in staff. A letter published in The Howdenshire Gazette on Friday 25th January 1895 expresses concern:

"To turn out from home at all hours, in all kinds of weather for the purpose of earning a couple of shillings per day, which hundreds of men do regularly is a deplorable state of affairs which does not need other exactions to aggravate. It is to be hoped that the capitalists concerned in the amalgamation will remember that while they have their rights and privileges, they also have reasonable regard for the workman who helps to keep up their incomes."

This amalgamation does indeed proceed. The Goole Steam Shipping Company takes over the Yorkshire Coal and Steamship Company, and the Humber Steam Shipping Company. The Company purchases the three steamers owned by the Humber Steam Shipping Company. This must have made quite a significant difference in the competition at Goole, now between the significantly larger Goole Steam Shipping Company and the Bennett Steam Ship Company.

One of the Bennett steamers is in the news, in January of this year, when another 'incident' occurs at Goole docks. This is reported in the Howdenshire Gazette on Friday 25th January 1895 (see transcription *figure 72*). This must have been quite alarming for those on board the Burma at the time.

1895 also brings with it truly severe cold weather. The following week The Goole Times, Friday 1st February reports:

"THE CONDITION OF THE RIVER OUSE – The keen frost and repeated downfalls of snow have given the river Ouse quite an artic appearance, and it is with difficulty that the waters can be navigated. The keel traffic from Hull to Goole has been stopped, by the withdrawal of the Whitton lightships steamships are unable to make the passage except in daylight. Yesterday morning several steamers arrived and departed; but the ss Hollinside, of Newcastle, which had discharged a cargo of copper ore, steamed as far as Goole Reach but could proceed no further owning to the impact of ice, and had to return to the locks. Should the snow and frost continue, the river will assume a more serious aspect, and probably be blocked."

A LUNATIC ABROAD IN GOOLE
HE OWNED ALL THE GOOLE STEAMERS
At the Goole Police Court on Monday before Mr Councillor Huntington and Mr H.C.F. Hartman – William George Todd (18), of Gilberdyke, was charged with being a wandering lunatic. PC Wilson said that about seven o'clock on Saturday morning he saw this young man behaving in a very disorderly manner on Goole docks. He went among the coal trimmers on board the Burma and when a number of sailors wanted to get on board, he met them with a hand-spike and threatened them, saying they were foreigners. He took charge of him and brought him to the police station. Dr Blair gave evidence to the effect that he had made an examination of the prisoner, and he believed him to be insane. Dr Blair (to prisoner): Do not the steamers in Goole belong to you? Prisoner: Yes, they all do, and there's no steamers going out till there's some alteration. In answer to the magistrates, prisoner said his name was Wm Todd, or "Bill Todd if you like." Mr Huntington, pointing to Mr Wilson, said that gentleman would take care of the prisoner. Prisoner: That's right, sir. It was decided to send him to the asylum at Wakefield.

Figure 72

The extent of this severe weather on the sea can be seen in this photograph of Woolwich Reach from Charlton 1894 into 1895 *figure 73*. As seen, the hazards to operations for the shipping world at this time are many and varied, from the sinking of 70 'Tom Puddings', to threatening individuals, and extreme weather.

Figure 73

On Wednesday, the 30th January, John Bennett attends a meeting as part of a deputation of the Goole Shipowners Association to discuss the need to increase the number of coal tipping appliances at the docks. This meeting takes place immediately before the open meeting of the Goole Urban District Council. After one hour, they pass a resolution, to request that the Council should appoint a delegation to join with the Goole Shipowners Association, in making an application to the Lancashire and Yorkshire Railway Company, and the Aire and Calder Navigation, for increased facilities for loading coal. Obviously the growth in the shipping trade to and from the port of Goole, and the ever increasing number of vessels put into service is more than the current facilities could handle. For these business men, a need to turn around their vessels quickly is paramount to their success and ultimately, profit.

The same newspaper, Friday 1st February 1895, reports a tragedy of enormous magnitude; an event that must have rocked the shipping world. The report states that a vessel known to the port of Goole appears to have caused this accident. The heading reads 'A Goole Trader Sinks An Atlantic

Steamer'. The story is as follows:

"An awful catastrophe occurred in the North Sea on Wednesday morning. In the darkness of the early morning the North German-Lloyd steamer Elbe, 4,500 tons, from Bremen to Southampton, and thence to new York, was proceeding about fifty miles off Lowestoft when she was run into by a vessel, which struck her just abaft the engines and broke a huge hole in her side. The water rushed in, in a flood, and the steamer sank in about 20 minutes. She had on board 240 passengers and a crew of 160 and only five of the passengers and 15 of the crew escaped. There was but time to get out three of the boats, and of these one was distinctly swamped. Another, with the 20 survivors, was five-and-a-half hours on the sea before she was seen and its occupants brought to Lowestoft. Of the other vessel no trace was seen after the collision."

The account speaks of the vessel responsible:

"...there seems no doubt that the vessel which ran into the Elbe was the Crathie. The Crathie was a steamer of about 500 tons register, and was generally employed in the coal carrying trade, but she had recently been engaged in running between Rotterdam and Aberdeen. The Craithie has frequently been at Goole, and only about a month ago was engaged taking stone from Goole to Hamburg."

It is not hard to imagine the shock and devastation this must have brought to those in the shipping world and the public in general. The loss of life to such magnitude must have left people reeling. When the story unfolded, it appeared that a helmsman and a lookout on board the Craithie had been sharing the watch. In order to warm himself by a stove, the lookout went below, leaving the helmsman alone on the bridge. The Elbe had seen the small freighter heading straight for their course but could not itself change course due to the 'rule of the road' at sea. The resultant fatal collision brought

106

about changes in the rules for shipping. All of the shipping companies would have been responsible for ensuring that they adhered to these new regulations, and the Bennett Steamship Company would have been well aware of the aftermath of this awful tragedy. The vessel involved was very alike those owned by Bennetts.

On Saturday, the 9th February 1895, the Bennett Steamship Company witnesses a serious incident on board the Malta in the 'Quai Chanzy' at Boulogne. Having arrived in the port on Friday morning, the cargo is offloaded during Saturday with the exception of the coal and some barrels of creosote. In the afternoon, several barrels unloaded, one falls from the grip of the hoist, back into the bilges underneath the limber boards. At 8:30 in the evening, a number of sailors go down into the hold, taking with them a lamp. A terrible explosion occurs. Two or three of the labourers were extremely badly burned around the face and head. Some creosote then caught fire which was eventually extinguished with sand, and creosote cleared from under all but one limber board. A short time later, upon taking a 'riding light' (with a covered in flame) down below deck, another explosion occurs when they lift the last limber board. Three sailors (all from Goole) were very badly burned. A French sailor received serious injuries, having dreadful burns to his body, arms and legs. Dr Granger Brown attended all of the Goole sailors on their arrival back at Goole.

The company must have found this episode terribly shocking, and no doubt provide a great deal of assistance to those injured and their families. John Bennett had a reputation as a kind and caring person, and I am sure he would have visited these men in their homes.

Between 1894-5, the Hydra leaves the Bennett fleet. In Lloyds Register 1895-6, entry no 1011, the Hydra has now been named the Stettin. A company named VestlandskeLloyd now owns this vessel with her registered port Bergen, Norway.

Spirits lift at the Bennett Steamship Company, however, with the arrival of a new steamer a few weeks later. John Bennett commissions the ss Corea from a local shipbuilder – Messrs Earle's Shipbuilding and Engineering Company Limited of Hull see *figure 74*. Built in yard number 393, her dimensions were – 210 feet by 31 feet by 14 feet 4 inches. She was of class 'steel 100 A1' and her gross tons 776. Her registered ship number is 98398. The full specifications of the vessel from Lloyds Register can be seen in *figure 75*. Arthur Frederick Bennett is at this time engaged in the engine works drawing office at Earles, having served a five year apprenticeship with them from 1887.

The Goole Times reports the arrival of the Corea on the 15th March 1895:

"On Saturday Messrs Earle's Shipbuilding and Engineering Company, Limited, Hull, made an addition to the fleet of the Bennett Steamship Company, Limited, of Goole, in the shape of the steamer Corea, a steel screw steamer, which they launched on the afternoon of that day. She is 210 ft long, 31ft beam, and 13ft 8ins. depth, being built to Lloyd's highest class and is intended for the Goole and Boulogne trade. The Corea is a fine-looking vessel of the raised quarter-deck type, having a short bridge amidships, and top-gallant forecastle. Water ballast is provided in the main and after holds, and strong web frames are fitted so as to enable hold beams to be dispensed with, and thereby leaving the entire hold space clear for the reception of cargo. The hatchways are of large size, and the derricks and cargo gear exceptionally strong, while powerful winches are also provided for the rapid handling of cargo. The bridge is fitted up for the accommodation of the captain and twelve passengers, with dining saloon in polished woods, state-room, and all necessary conveniences, the entrance being from a deck-house above, which contains also a chart-room and steering house. The officers' and engineers' quarters are situated aft under the quarter-deck and those of the crew in the forecastle.

There is a powerful combined hand and steam steering gear amidships, and suitable screw gear aft. The vessel will be schooner rigged, having two pole masts and fore and aft canvas. Her machinery, also constructed by Earle's Company, will consist of a set of triple expansion engines of great power and of most recent design, steam for which will be supplied by two steel cylindrical boilers made for a working pressure of 160 lbs per square inch. The christening ceremony was performed by Miss E Bennett in the presence of a large company of guests, which included Mr and Mrs John Bennett, sen., Mr J Bennett, jun., Mr A and the Misses Bennett, Captain Ingleby, Mr and Mrs Henry Bennett, Mr A.E. Seaton, Mr Frank H Pearson and others."

What an exciting day this must have been for 19 year old Edith. As the Bennetts had their own jetty to the rear of Grove House in Goole, this may have been the setting for the 'christening'. It is easy to imagine their pride at having the new vessel anchored (possibly) at the bottom of the garden with all the guests milling around. Judging by the extreme cold of the past month people may not have lingered for long, perhaps the Bennetts provided refreshments inside the house for those invited guests. Mr A.E. Seaton was the General Manager at Earles and under whom Arthur Frederick had carried out his apprenticeship.

In the shipping lists for Goole, the Corea makes her first official sailing on the 13th April, under the command of Captain Ingleby, loaded with a cargo of 'goods' bound for Boulogne. In the month since her delivery, she was probably undergoing the work to equip her with the schooner rigging mentioned in the earlier newspaper report. The Corea seems to have been synonymous with the port of Boulogne. Albert Chatelle writes in his history of the company:

"She sailed like a Witch with the regularity of a Liner of the largest class and it was always with pleasure that the

Employees of Bennett's on seeing her leave the Bassin Loubet would say "There's the Corea leaving"."

The photograph in *figure 76* shows the Corea sailing into the port of Boulogne. The captains again make a 'reshuffle' with Captain Ingleby, the company's senior captain, taking the helm of their new vessel.

Back to the family, *figure 77* shows the occasion of Arthur Frederick Bennett's marriage to Constance Charlotte (Connie) Kirkby in 1895. Arthur's three sisters, Edith Elizabeth, Isabel (Belle) and the younger girl (at the front), Mary Elleanor (Mopsy) all on the right of the picture, are bridesmaids. In the same year 1895, which has so far brought mixed stories, good and bad, there is tragedy again for the Bennett family. Sarah Ann (Sallie) Bennett, who married on August 1st of the previous year, gives birth to a son on July 31st. He only lives for six minutes, and the birth leaves Sarah Ann desperately ill. She dies 19th August 1895, at the age of 24. This is ten years since John's daughter Annie Charlotte died in the summer of 1885. A special column in The Goole Times of Friday 23rd August gives an account of Sarah Ann's death:

"DEATH OF MRS. WALTER BRUNYEE, OF EASTOFT
The death took place on Monday afternoon, at Eastoft, of Mrs Walter Brunyee, daughter of Mr John Bennett, of Grove House, Goole, ship-owner. The deceased lady, who has only been married a little over twelve months, gave birth prematurely to a child, which only lived about six minutes, on July 31st. Instead of improving, her condition became gradually worse, and in addition to the local doctor (Dr Cranage, of Crowle), the services of two physicians were requisitioned. Two trained nurses have also been in attendance, and everything possible was done to bring about her recovery, but she died as stated. Mrs Brunyee was a sister to Mrs Todd, of Brough. A number of ships in the docks are flying their flags half-mast high. The deceased lady, who was

Figure 74

Figure 75

Ship No	98398
Name	Corea
Description	Steel Screw Schooner
Master	J Ingleby – 95
Tonnage	Gross 776, Under deck 567, net 300
Dimensions	Length – 210.0 Breadth – 31.0 Depth – 13.6
Engines	T.3Cy.19", 32" & 52"-36" 160lb 80lb 170 NHP 2SB, 4rf, GS84, HS2670 by Earles Co Ltd Hull
Builder	Earle's S B & E Co Ltd Hull
Built	1895 4mo
Owner	Bennett Steam Ship Co Ltd
Registered port	Goole
Port of survey	Hull
Class	100 A1 (built under special survey)

111

Figure 76

Figure 77

only about 24 years of age, was married at the same time as her sister, Mrs Todd of Brough, the event being made a double one."

As seen from the newspaper account, the port of Goole shows its respect with a number of ships flying flags at half mast. John, deeply saddened by the loss of both his daughter and his grandson, could not foresee that more tragedy is in store for the family just a few weeks later. Mary Ann, John Bennett's beloved second wife dies on the 28th October, aged 51 years. The Goole Times reports this on the 1st November 1895, with a special column in the newspaper covering the funeral. This coverage demonstrates the significance of the Bennett family in the town of Goole.

"THE FUNERAL OF MRS BENNETT – The remains of this deceased lady, the wife of Mr John Bennett, Grove House, Old Goole, were interred in the family vault at Whitgift Churchyard on Wednesday afternoon, the officiating clergyman being the Rev W Williams, vicar, assisted by the Rev W H Carr, vicar of Goole. The relatives and mourners were as follows: - First carriage, Mr John Bennett, the Misses Bennett, Mr Arthur Bennett, and Master Bennett; second carriage, Mr and Mrs William Sykes and Miss Sykes (Ousefleet), the Rev W H Carr, Mr Todd, and the professional nurse; third carriage, Mr J Bennett, jun., Mr and Mrs H T Bennett, and Mr and Mrs H Wilson; fourth carriage, Mrs Robt. Sykes, Mr Henry Bennett, Mr W Bennett, and Mr R Sykes, jun. Amongst other mourners were Mr and Mrs G England, Mr and Mrs W Brunyee, Mr Ireland, jun., and others. The coffin, which was of polished oak, was made by Mr Hutchinson, Old Goole, and the general arrangements were satisfactorily carried out by Mr J Huntington."

For the Bennett family, 1895 is a year of highs and lows. The town of Goole is changing at a tremendous pace. In 1895, there are 177 vessels registered at the port, and a net tonnage recorded of 23,328. Duties received in the custom house amounted to £25,700. Further information can be found about the Bennett Steamship Company in the Crew Agreements of 1895/6. On 6th May 1895, the master of the China moves to join the Burma. Several crew members from the Burma transfer to join the China. The voyages made by the China at this time are mainly between London and Boulogne. The master of the China in 1896 was R Goodworth of 59 Carter Street Goole. In 1895, the masters of the India are William Denby and William Aaron. Engaged in the 'home trade' it is making voyages between Goole and Boulogne and London and Boulogne. The masters of the Malta in 1895 are J Colbridge and S L Ingleby.[36]

1896 sees the erection of the new Goole Market Hall, mentioned earlier in this story, designed by Mr H T Tennant, architect, of Pontefract at the cost of £4,000. Situated at the junction of Boothferry Road and Estcourt Terrace, this building still survives today.

On the 29th October 1896, an auction takes place of live and dead farm stock at Key Field Farm Swinefleet. This includes 25 horses, 23 beast, 20 pigs, poultry, and 40 'couple' of fowl.[37] John Bennett gives instruction for this sale since he has now leased this farm.

Kelly's Directory of 1897, details some of the industries found in Goole. Several iron foundries and engineering works are in operation, and on the canal side are the works of the Pure Tillage and Cattle Food Company. There are also shipbuilding yards, sail-lofts, roperies and the timber yards of E Maude and Sons, and Illingworth, Ingham and Company.

In this year, a collision occurs involving the Corea, the flagship vessel of the Bennett Steamship Company, as reported in The Goole Weekly Times, Friday 12th March 1897:
"THE SS COREA IN COLLISION – On Friday the steamer Corea, of Goole, from Boulogne, with a general cargo, collided

with the steamer Medway, of London, while the latter was lying at anchor in Hull Roads. The Corea had several plates damaged on her port side amid-ships. The Corea proceeded to Goole, where she discharged. The damage to the Medway was unimportant, but she lost anchor and chain."

The local directories from 1892 show that Bennetts were at number 11 Nelson Street, Hull, sharing this address with two other companies, Hagcrup & Company shipowners, and Kiveton Park Coal Company, Colliery Owners. The map from 1913 in *figure 78* shows Nelson Street just behind Victoria Pier and the Ferry and Boat Docks.

On the occasion of what appears to be another family wedding (unidentified) *figure 79*, the Grove House extension mentioned earlier in this story can clearly be seen. The stone lintel bears John Bennetts' initials and the year 1889. The brickwork on the right looks slightly different to that of the original building. It is extremely difficult to pick out the bride and groom even in this photograph.

In June 1898, Isabel marries the Reverend Hugh Seymour Tupholme. In March, they leave Goole for a curacy at Gargrave a beautiful village in Airedale on the borders of Wharfedale and the moors.

This year also sees yet another addition to the Bennett Line fleet the ss Syria also built by Earle's Shipbuilding, Hull, from yard number 440. The Syria weighed 749 gross tons *figure 80*. The Bennett Steamship Company fleet now comprises of six vessels. The specifications of the vessel from Lloyds Register can be seen in *figure 81*.

By the close of the century, John Bennett has well and truly established himself as a prominent figure in the public and business arena.

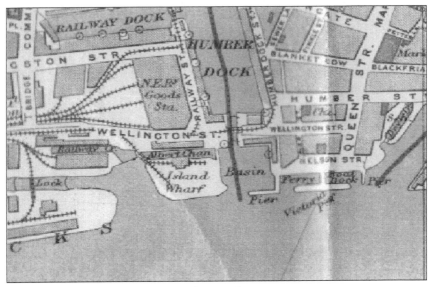

Figure 78

Figure 79

Figure 80

Figure 81

Ship No	104222
Name	Syria
Description	Steel Screw Schooner
Master	J Ingleby 76-98
Tonnage	282 net 781 gross 567 under deck
Dimensions	Length – 210.0 Breadth – 31.0 Depth – 13.6
Engines	T3Cy19",32" & 52"-36" 180lb 175 NHP 2 SB 4cf, GS84, HS 2670 By Earles Co Ltd Hull
Builder	Earles Co Ltd Hull
Built	1898
Owner	Bennett Steam Ship Co Ltd
Registered port	Goole
Port of survey	Hull, Goole
Class	100 A1 (built under special survey)

The publication, "The Siren & Shipping Illustrated", features him in their 'headlight' article Wednesday 27th September 1899. This publication also features a column *figure 82* about John Bennett listing some of his principle undertakings. These include chairman of the Local Board, president of the Chamber of Commerce, chairman of the Goole Engineering and Shipbuilding Company Ltd., chairman of the Goole and Pure Tillage Company Ltd., director of the Gas and Water Company and one of the sub-Pilot Commissioners of the Humber. A lovely engraving of John Bennett features on the front cover *figure 83*.

AND SHIPPING.   SEPT. 27, 1899.

JOHN BENNETT. Esq.

ALTHOUGH now well-known both in this country and France, as chairman of the Bennett Steamship Company, of Goole, our this week's "Headlight" did not originally engage in business as a shipowner. That departure he made in 1875, previous to which time he was known as a merchant and importer, doing an extensive business—in fruit especially. In the year we have just mentioned, he first turned his attention to the industry with which his name is now so well-known, establishing regular steamship communication between Goole and Calais. Shortly afterwards he commenced a Goole and Ostend service of steamers. The former line was only continued as originally established for some twelve months, the French port, in 1876, being changed from Calais to Boulogne-sur-Mer, that harbour possessing greater opportunities for the building up of a profitable service than the former. The wisdom of the change was apparent at the outset, for whilst one sailing a week had sufficed for the Calais trade, two every seven days were necessary for the Boulogne service. Naturally, the increased trade did not come entirely of itself; it was considerably increased by the untiring energy of our "Headlight," supported by his two sons—Mr. John Bennett, Junr., and Mr. Robert Bennett—both of whom rendered most valuable assistance. The undertaking continued to prosper exceedingly, until, in 1890, it was deemed desirable to transfer it to a limited company—the present Bennett Steamship Company, Limited—the shares of which were all privately subscribed, the greater proportion being retained by our "Headlight" and the members of his family. Shortly after the formation of the Limited Company, the scope of the business was enlarged by the acquisition of a steamer service between London and Boulogne, and *vice versa*. The two services have now, as they have had from the beginning, the personal attention of our "Headlight;" whilst Mr. John Bennett, Junr., acts as manager at Goole, Mr. Robt. Bennett occupying a similar position at Boulogne. The result of this careful supervision is evidenced by the highly flourishing position of the Bennett Steamship Co. to-day. The opinion held of the methods by which the Company is operated, was shown by the remark of a well-known shipping M.P. a short time ago. "If you desire to send goods from England to France," he said, "Goole is the place, and Bennett the man." Seeing that each line has now three services per week, performed by steamers specially built for the trade, it is evident that the eulogy was well merited. Whilst Mr. Bennett has been thus successful and energetic in business, he has still found time to take a deep interest in the public life of the port and town of Goole, the chief undertakings in the town having benefited from his assistance. The list would occupy more space than we have at our disposal; but amongst the public offices our "Headlight" has occupied was the chairmanship of the Local Board, a position he held for a number of years. He was, for an equally lengthened period, a successful president of the Chamber of Commerce. Besides such honorary offices as these, our "Headlight" is closely identified with many of the most important commercial enterprises of Goole. Thus, we find him chairman of the Goole Engineering and Shipbuilding Company, Ltd.; chairman of the Goole Pure Tillage Company, Ltd.; director of the Gas and Water Company, etc. He is also one of the sub-Pilot Commissioners of the Humber.

Figure 82

Registered as a Newspaper.

The SYREN AND Shipping

A WEEKLY ILLUSTRATED JOURNAL

Subscription: Post Free in the United Kingdom, 15s. per annum; Abroad, 17s. per annum.

VOL. XIII.—No. 161. WEDNESDAY, SEPTEMBER 27, 1899. THREEPENCE.

JOHN BENNETT, Esq.

Goole.

[See page 110.]

Figure 83

119

Chapter 6
The Dawn of a New Century –The End of an Era

Figure 84

Figure 84 is a photograph of John Bennett, probably taken sometime around the turn of the century, as I would estimate his age as early sixties. For the Bennett Steamship Company, it would appear that this was a boom time. Albert Chatelle writes in his history of the company:

"In 1900, now that the Bennett Company is in full activities the tonnage rose to 25,047,000 kgs fruit, 12,825,000 kgs vegetables and 83,724,000 kgs potatoes. Finally the traffic of natural flowers sent in complete wagons from the region of Nice and destined for the great markets of London had made its appearance and in this same year – 1900 there were nearly 2,000 of these wicker flower baskets which were transported at great speed through our port transforming the steamers of the Bennett Steamship Co – also Pierre-Lot – into a ship of flowers".

The company operations can be seen advertised on one of their envelopes *figure 85* posted 28th March 1900 to a Monsieur Panin, Boulogne-sur-Mer, France. They proudly inform that they are "Taking goods to and from all parts of France, Germany, Switzerland, Italy." Details of some of the goods transported by the company are shown later in this chapter. Around this time, a Joseph Sutton becomes Manager at Boulogne for a period of five years, after previously working for the London Northwestern Railway and later the Lancashire & Yorkshire Railway.

"On certain days in August 1901", declared Mr Ferdinand Ferjon, president of the Chamber of Commerce at a conference, "we saw arrive in Boulogne up to 7 or 8 special trains loaded with 66,000 baskets of fruit which were despatched the same day, whilst the empty baskets returning, were also sent back. The number of cases were reckoned to be about 7 million per year." Une Page De L'Histoire De Notre Port from La Voix Maritime, 25th September 1975.[38]

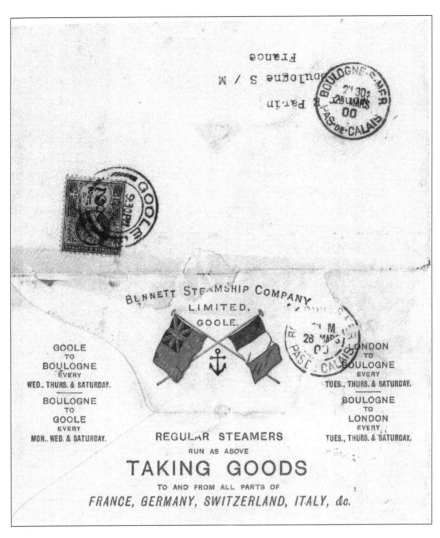

Figure 85

The census taken on the 31st March earlier that year (1901) shows the family spread far and wide. At the family home, Grove House, on that evening, John Bennett now a widower age 65 is at home with his daughter Edith Elizabeth age 25, visitor Ingham Spinks, a carpet merchant (later to marry Edith), and four servants *figure 86*.

His eldest son John is still living with his wife Elizabeth and family at 19 Heber Terrace, Goole, *figure 87*. Second eldest, Herbert Thomas is now living with his wife Mary and family at Potter Grange, Airmyn, *figure 88*. In 1926 Herbert and his family move to 'Hafodty' at Ruddington near Nottingham. John's daughter Mary Adelaide is living at 56 Alderney Street, St George Hanover Square in London with her husband Daniel Hewitt Todd and their young family *figure 89*. The birthplaces of their children show that they are all born in or around Hull, Yorkshire the youngest child one year previously. They had clearly moved south quite recently. It is likely, looking at Daniel's profession, that he may have had some work with the Bennett Steamship Company down at their London operation. The whereabouts of Robert and Albert, children from John's marriage to Sarah Ann, are not known. However, since Robert is in charge of French operations it may be assumed he is living in France at this time. Edith's diary indicates that 'Hal' is sailing faraway oceans.

Where are the children of John Bennett and Mary Ann Sykes? Their eldest son Arthur Frederick, who as seen previously, married Connie, is found on board the Navy vessel, HMS Duke of Wellington, at Portsea and Landport, Portsmouth. Given as 'crew' aged 29, his occupation is that of engineer. At this time, he was manager for Earle's Shipbuilding and Engineering Company and in charge of the fitting out of vessels in the Admiralty section of the company. This vessel, once famous flagship of Sir Charles Napier, is at this time relegated to harbour service as one of the depot ships for berthing the men of the Portsmouth Dockyard Reserve. Eldest daughter Isabel and her husband the Reverend Hugh S Tupholme are with their family still living at Gargrave on the borders of Wharfedale *figure 90*. They later move to Kettering in 1905, to St.Leonard, Bedford in 1910 and to Peckham, London in 1919. Finally in 1923 they move to Orlingbury, where they live for 23 years until Hugh's death. None of their children marry. John Bentley Bennett (Jack) has not been located on this census. In 1902, he lives at 15 East Parade, Goole, with the occupation of Shipping Clerk. John Bentley Bennett buys Manor Cottage, Goole, with its 7 acres on 24th March 1920. The Aire and Calder Navigation company founded the town of Goole in 1826. John and Ellen Lister, Manager of York City and County Banking Company occupied the house originally named "Mannure Cottage" and once owned by the Earl of Beverley. The Listers made extensive alterations turning the house to face north and adding a new wooden staircase, dining room downstairs and drawing room upstairs. Manor Cottage, probably built at the end of the 17th century, began life as a small labourer's cottage/shooting lodge with two rooms linked by a ladder and trapdoor. It is on land originally owned by the famous Percy family (Dukes of Northumberland) who were involved in the Goole area in schemes to channel the River Don and drain the marshland. The 18th century saw more extensions to Manor Cottage with the addition of a large kitchen and stone staircase leading to three small bedrooms. Further extensive alterations take place around 1835. John Bentley Bennett installs a bathroom and toilet and lives there until 1944.

The youngest child of all, Mary Eleanor, is following in another family tradition, that of education for girls. She is found at the Ladies School 'Walderneath' on Cornwall Road, Harrogate not far from where her older half-sisters attended Belvedere Ladies School on Victoria Avenue. Mary Eleanor is 15 years old at this time, and a total of 31 pupils are living in from as far away as Scotland and Wales. The joint Proprietors of this establishment are Elizabeth A Blythe, a single woman aged 64, and Elisa Koch single aged 58 and of German origin. Five teachers are in residence – Miss Blythe Teacher of Music (possibly related to the proprietor), Miss Anderson Teacher of Mathematics, Miss Bomford Teacher of English, a Teacher of French, and Miss Knowlson Teacher of English.

On the 6th August 1901, Edith Elizabeth marries Ingham Spinks at Goole Parish Church. Reverend Hugh Tupholme (her

Figure 86 - 1901 Census – Goole

Abode	Person	Relationship To Head	Cond*	Age		Rank, Profession Or Occupation	Where Born
				Male	Female		
Grove House	John Bennett	Head	Widr	65		Chairman, Bennett SS Co	Adlingfleet
	Edith Elizabeth Bennett	Dau	S		25		Lancs, Southport
	Ingham Spinks	Visitor	S	27		Carpet Merchant	Yorks, Ludo
	Louisa Robertson	Serv	S		30	Cook (Domestic)	London
	Sarah Ann Moon	Serv	S		28	Waitress Domestic	Yorks, Pickering
	Alice Smith	Serv	S		19	Housemaid Domestic	Yorks, Goole
	Mary Alice Coates	Serv	S		16	Kitchenmaid Domestic	Yorks, Goole

*Condition   Widr=Widower   S=Single

125

Figure 87 - 1901 Census – Goole

Abode	Person	Relationship To Head	Cond*	Age		Rank, Prof. Or Occ.	Where Born
				Male	Female		
19 Heber Terrace	John Bennett	Head	M	39		Manager Steamship Co	Yorks, Adlingfleet
	Elizabeth Bennett	Wife	M		36		Yorks, Goole
	Elsie Bennett	Dau	S		9		Yorks, Goole
	John Bennett	Son	S	5			Yorks, Goole
	Catherine Ainger	Visitor	M		45		Renfrew, Scotland
	Lena Thompson	Servant	S		19	Servant Domestic	Yorks, Goole

*Condition   M=Married   S=Single

Figure 88 - 1901 Census - Goole

Abode	Person	Relationship To Head	Cond*	Age		Rank, Profession Or Occupation	Where Born
				Male	Female		
Potter Grange	Herbert T Bennett	Head	M	37		Farmer Potato Merchant	Yorks, Adlingfleet
	Mary Bennett	Wife	M		37		Liverpool
	Robert G Bennett	Son	S	7			Yorks, Swinefleet
	Marion Bennett	Dau	S		5		Yorks, Swinefleet
	Martha England	Visitor	S		26		Yorks, Goole
	Annie Huntington	Serv	S		20	Housemaid (Domestic)	Yorks, Goole
	Alice Emmerson	Serv	S		25	Cook (Domestic)	Yorks, Eastoft

*Condition   M=Married   S=Single

127

Figure 89 – 1901 Census – London

Abode	Person	Relationship To Head	Cond*	Age		Rank, Prof. Or Occ.	Where Born
				Male	Female		
56 Alderney Street	Daniel Todd	Head	M	30		Mechanical Engineer	France (Eng. Subject)
	Mary A Todd	Wife	M		28		Yorks, Adlingfleet
	Gordon H Todd	Son	S	5			Yorks, Hull
	Gladys M Todd	Dau	S		5		Yorks, Hull
	George S B Todd	Son	S	3			Yorks, Brough
	Daniel G B Todd	Son	S	1			Yorks, Hull

*Condition   M=Married   S=Single

128

Figure 90 - 1901 Census - Gargrave

Abode	Person	Relationship To Head	Cond*	Age		Rank, Prof. Cr Occ.	Where Born
				Male	Female		
Old Hall Cottage	Hugh S Tupholme	Head	M	31		Clergyman Church of England	Middlesex, Ealing
	Isabel Tupholme	Wife	M		27		Lancs, Lytham
	Dorothy Ann Tupholme	Dau	S		1		Yorks, Gargrave
	Micheal J Tupholme	Son	S	8mths			Yorks, Gargrave
	Annie Maud Northing	Serv	S		19	Domestic	Lincs, Kirton in Lindsey
	Kate Austin	Serv	S		17		Northamptonshire Hessington

*Condition   M=Married   S=Single

brother-in-law) officiates at the marriage. Ingham's father Albert Ingham Spinks founded Denby and Spinks luxury furniture store which later had branches in Leeds, Harrogate, and Johannesburg. Ingham becomes chairman of Denby and Spinks.

Back on the business front in the Goole Times of Friday, October 11th 1901, the story continues: "We note with pleasure that orders have been placed, by the builders, with Messrs. Webster and Bickerton, of Phoenix Foundry, Goole, for three of their improved type of horizontal steam winches for the new steamer now building on the Clyde for Messrs. The Bennett Steam Shipping Company, of Goole." The new vessel in question will be mentioned later.

In 1901 John Bennett sells most of his estates in Reedness and Swinefleet consisting of various properties and land. A breakdown of these properties can be seen in *figure 91*. According to a handwritten note by John Bentley Bennett this estate sells for £51,400 on the 1st October 1901.[39] This translates to approximately £4million in today's value. The buyer, J H Lock Esquire, is the nominee of the Denaby and Cadeby Collieries.

Figure 91

	Acres	Roods	Perches
Keyfield Farm	184	1	15
Highfields Farm	188	1	0
Mount Pleasant Farm	169	3	36
Kings Causeway Farm	94	3	7
Agricultural Holdings Swinefleet	23	1	21
2 closes of arable land moors	17	0	0
Capital smallholding Swinefleet	14	3	12
Ryefield House 1 mile from Reedness	8	1	32
Upper Sands	6	2	9
Pair of cottages Swinefleet			
Drainhead	0	3	36
Warps Grass Close	1	0	11
Ryefield Pasture	0	2	19
2 arable Middle Sands	0	1	29
The Hob & River Frontage Swinefleet	0	3	7

Figure 92

Figure 93

John Bennett establishes his Paris office sometime between the turn of the century and this point in the story. The Paris office was at 120 Rue Lafayette. The postcard *figure 92* shows a view of Rue Lafayette probably taken early 1900s (certainly before the age of the motorcar). Around 1902, John Bennett purchases Chamberlains Wharf on the River Thames used by the company's steamers, for the purpose of establishing a separate business outside of the steamship company. The acquisition of additional land together with the construction of new buildings, enabled this to be considerably extended, and the pier, which connects it to the river, enlarged. *Figure 93* shows the view from Chamberlain's Wharf looking towards Tower Bridge around 1905. In the Post Office London Conveyance Directory for 1899, there is a listing for Chamberlain's Wharf Limited at 15 and 27 Tooley Street. The managing director at that time is Edward Bealey. It goes on to state that steamers of the Bennett Line depart 3 times a week for Boulogne. As seen from Company advertisements, the location of the Bennett Company office is 15 Tooley Street. Perhaps it made sense combining operations. An old map of the Thames shows the location of numerous wharves and this section *figure 94* includes Chamberlain's Wharf.

John Bentley Bennett marries Barbara Phillips in the latter part of 1901.

On the 11th January 1902, John Bennett writes his will again, this time witnessed by the family solicitor George England and George Hunt, secretary to the Bennett Steamship Company. How he leaves his estate follows later in this chapter.

A postcard advertising the Bennett Line, *figure 95*, shows the loading of locomotives onto the deck of one of the vessels. The next new vessel joins the Bennett fleet in 1902, and will go on to carry such a cargo. She is the ss Mopsa, *figure 96*, and perhaps John named this vessel after the pet name given to his youngest daughter Mary Eleanor - 'Mopsy'.

132

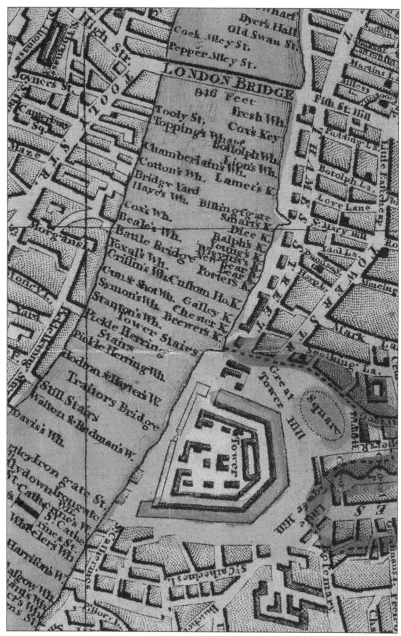

Figure 94

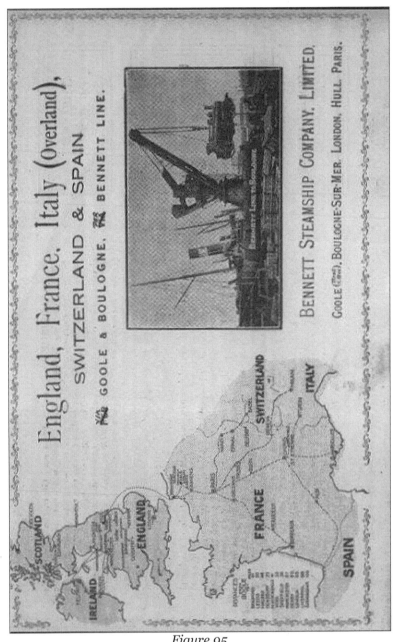

Figure 95

Figure 96

Figure 97

Ship No	114033
Name	Mopsa
Description	Steel Screw Schooner
Master	W Denby 90 – 02
Tonnage	1200 Total – gross 885, Under deck 664, net 385
Dimensions	Length 225.0 Breadth – 33.1 Depth – 13.6
Engines	T3Cy19",32" & 52"-36" 180lb 187 NHP 2 SB 4cf, G582, HS 3044 Muir & Houston Ld, Gls
Builder	Murdoch & Murray Pt Glasgow
Built	1902
Owner	Bennett Steam Ship Co Ltd
Registered port	Goole
Class	100 A1

Built by Murdoch & Murray of Glasgow (yard 187) her gross tonnage is 885. Launched on Wednesday 23rd April 1902, her registered ship number is 114033. The specifications of the vessel from Lloyds Register can be seen in *figure 97*. The following year 1903 sees the arrival of yet another ship to the Bennett fleet, the ss Africa *figure 98*. This is the second vessel commissioned from the shipbuilder Earle of Hull (yard 481). Her registered ship number is 114036, and her gross tons 1038. The specifications of the vessel from Lloyds Register can be seen in *figure 99*.

In 1903, the Goole Steam Shipping Company build new offices opposite St. John's Church, at the southern end of Church Street, Goole, with a frieze of sailing ships, and not a steamboat in sight, above the main entrance. Presumably the numerous shipping companies can no longer fit into Bank Chambers.

The year 1904 marks the end of an era for the Bennett family, when John Bennett passes away at 9:20 on Sunday evening, the 14th February. Apparently John becomes confined to his home, Grove House, two weeks prior to his death. The family summoned the services of three doctors, his own Doctor, Blair, and Doctors Edison and Barrs of Leeds. The newspaper report states that he dies from cerebral disease. The Goole Times of Friday, 19th February 1904 gives extensive coverage of his death and subsequent funeral. The report begins:

"One would have to go a long way back to find an event that has created so much mournful interest in the Ouse port as the funeral of the late Mr John Bennett, which took place in the quiet churchyard at Whitgift on Wednesday afternoon. It would be a hopeless task to endeavour to give a complete list of the names of those who were present to witness the departure of the cortege from Grove House, or even of those who were represented. Punctually at one o'clock two open vehicles with floral tributes, conspicuous amongst which were

Figure 98

Figure 99

Ship No	114036
Name	Africa
Description	Steel Screw Schooner
Master	W Denby
Tonnage	Gross 1038, Under deck 777, net 440
Dimensions	Length – 236.0 Breadth – 33.4 Depth – 14.0
Engines	T.3Cy.20", 34" & 56"-39" 180lb 80lb 233 NHP 2SB, 6rf, GS114, HS3890 by Earles Co Ltd Hull
Builder	Earle's Co Ltd Hull
Built	1903 4mo
Owner	Bennett Steam Ship Co Ltd
Registered port	Goole
Port of survey	Hull
Class	100 A1 (built under special survey)

two immense floral designs measuring six feet in length from Boulogne, emerged from the carriage drive of Grove House into the road; then followed the hearse containing the remains of one who all his life had been prominently connected with the port and the agricultural district in the immediate vicinity. The remains were followed by a long line of carriages and people on foot, seamen and landsmen were equally represented. Magistrates, councillor, professions and trades, commercial men and work people, dock officials and seamen, all followed in this silent procession which wended its way alongside the banks of the Ouse. At the urban boundary district limit many fell out and went on board the steamer Empress, which had been kindly placed at their disposal by the Goole and Hull Steam Packet Company, and then side by side on river and road, mourners and sympathisers followed the remains of the deceased gentleman to their last resting place."

The local newspaper names 140 mourners with the addition of the words "and numerous others". At the Sunday evening service, Father Pearson speaks to the congregation about John Bennett saying: "He was a man of good-will, of equable temper, kind-hearted and liberal, ever ready to help the needy when solicited".

In his will, John divides his shares in the Bennett Steamship Company as follows. Eldest son John receives 250 shares. To Herbert Thomas, Robert, Albert Edmund, Arthur Frederick, John Bentley, Isabel, and Edith Elizabeth, 150 shares each. Youngest daughter Mary Eleanor receives 200 shares. Mary Eleanor also receives £250 and Mary Adelaide £50. Two nieces receive £200 each, and to Thomas John Mason of Sheffield, Potato Merchant, Annie Mills and Wallace Dale, £200 each. His youngest daughter Mary Eleanor also inherits all "silver jewellery plate". Out of the realisation of his real and personal estate a sum of £3000 is to be invested for his daughter Mary Adelaide and her children. The remainder to be split into 20 equal parts; 3 parts to his eldest son John, 2 parts each to Herbert Thomas, Robert, John Bentley, Albert Edmund, Arthur Frederick, Isabel, Edith Elizabeth, and the remaining 3 parts to Mary Eleanor. John Bennett leaves Grove House and all its contents in trust for the sole use of Mary Eleanor.

The attendance list for the funeral names some of the captains. Captain Ingleby is now the Marine Superintendent; Captain Goodworth is on the Mopsa; Captain Aaron on the Burma.

The summer of 1904 also brings a local epidemic of diarrhoea, causing 57 deaths in the town, followed immediately by a measles outbreak. The child mortality rate soars. Poor sanitary conditions in the town exacerbate the situation. John Bennett himself campaigned to improve such conditions, when he had the position as chairman on the Goole and Hook Sanitary Committee.

On Tuesday June 21st 1904 at the Lowther Hotel the auction of the Grove House Estate takes place under the instruction of the executors of John Bennett.[40] The lots comprise:

Grove House - 5 acres, 2 roods and 7 perches.
A close of grassland - 2 acres 2 roods and 18 perches
(adjoining Grove House).
Decoy Farm, on the South Bank of the Dutch River,
between Goole and Rawcliffe Bridge.
20 lots of arable and grassland at Swinefleet, Reedness
and Whitgift - 74 acres, 31 perches.
Close of arable land on Doncaster Road, Haxey - 9 acres,
2 roods, 33 perches.

The sale catalogue fully describes Grove House as "a family residence for many years in the occupation of the owner the late John Bennett Esquire". An elaborate entrance hall leads into the house. There is a dining room, drawing room, breakfast room, library, and smoke room. For business use there is a strong room fitted with a Whitfields fire proof door measuring 6 feet by 2 feet. Further rooms include kitchen, butler's pantry, two store rooms, and a scullery. Upstairs are thirteen bedrooms, a bathroom and wc. It goes on to say that "the late owner quite recently expended a very large sum in improving and enlarging the residence, the costly interior decorations being in excellent taste and perfect condition. The pleasure grounds are charmingly laid out to a tennis court, an ornamental fountain, a conservatory and two greenhouses. The carriage drives and walks are asphalted. The kitchen garden is well stocked with wall, espalier and pyramid fruit trees in full bearing. The laundry is detached. There is a range of brick buildings comprising four stall stable, two stall stable, two coach houses, saddle room and four stall cow house. A large wood building in the paddock has been used as a concert and ballroom and there is a wood bicycle house. The excellent grass paddocks give access to the river Ouse which is approached through a fine avenue of beeches and grand old elms. There is a costly and substantial jetty projecting into the river giving access thereto at all states of the tide. The fountain, garden statuary, stone garden vases and wood swing are included in the sale. The purchaser will take, without valuation on completion of his purchase all the fruit and garden produce then growing except shrubs in tubs and plants in pots."

John Bentley Bennett makes a pencil note on the front of the catalogue that there was "no bidding". The reserve given as £3,300 has written against it £2,500, perhaps the highest bid. Another pencil note states "sold for £3000" 11th July 1904. This possibly referred just to Grove House. The adjoining grassland has £750 noted beside it. Decoy Farm has a pencil note "decided £1600" written against it. The various lots of arable land included in the sale can be seen in *figure 100*. Figures written alongside each lot in the catalogue would appear to be the transaction values. The previous spelling of "Key Field" has now altered to "Quay Field".

	Acres	Roods	Perches
Grass Land (£750)	2	2	18
Unspecified land (£450)	10	1	35
Quay Field Swinefleet (£220)	4	0	16
Quay Field Swinefleet (£120)	2	1	0
Quay Field Swinefleet (£190)	3	0	19
Quay Field Swinefleet (£110)	2	0	8
Lodge Field Swinefleet (£200)	3	3	28
Lodge Field Swinefleet (£50)	1	0	18
High West Moor Field Reedness (£100)	2	1	32
New Close Swinefleet (£130)	2	0	24
New Close Swinefleet (£600)	10	0	17
Lower Dunmires Swinefleet (no value given)	3	1	25
Dunmires Swinefleet (£40)	1	0	3
Longshores Swinefleet (£35)	0	2	18
Middle Sands Swinefleet (£50)	0	3	4
Longshores Swinefleet (£100)	2	2	33
Longshores & Long Ings Swinefleet (£55)	1	2	10
Dwelling home Underwoods Swinefleet (£150)	1	3	19
Warping Close Whitgift (£400)	10	2	10
Common Close Whitgift (£25)	9	3	32
One Cowgate in lanes of Whitgift			

Figure 100

Returning to the growth of the port of Goole, the Edwardian Medical Officer of Health and surgeon, Alexander McCorrell Erskine in his report of 1905, gives a summary of the economic fortunes of the town of Goole. "Being a seaport town, the chief occupation of the inhabitants is directly or indirectly associated with shipping, and consists of sailors, dock labourers, clerks, trades people, railway servants, and professional men, in addition to which there are shipbuilding yards, repairing yards, chemical works, tillage works, timber yards, flour mills, malt kilns, steam laundry, cabinet works, printing works, and Goole is the centre of a very important agricultural district. With regard to the progress of the town, the year has been one of activity. The shipbuilding yards have been fully occupied, trade in the main has been good, and building operations have been in progress all over the town." Alexander McCorrell Erskine was also a shareholder in the Bennett Steamship Company.

The company advertisement in the Goole Times Illustrated Almanack *figure 103* shows that Bennetts offer delivery to "all towns in France, Italy, Germany, Belgium, Switzerland & c". They are operating out of Goole, Hull, London, Paris and Boulogne. The French operations conducted from 20 Bourse du Commerce, Paris, Gare Maritime, Boulogne, also from 'Quai Vendoeuvre', Caen. By this time, the company has moved its base in Boulogne to 'Quai Maritime', from their original location at 'Quai Chanzy'. In 1905, Monsieur Georges Honoré who was at that time under-manager, replaces Robert Bennett as manager at Boulogne. Albert Chatelle writes:

"under the impulsion of M. George Honoré of whom it is useless to retrace a magnificent career, completely consecrated himself to the development of our port and the development of the Bennett Company which increased its activities ten times."

At this point in the story, various shipping notices feature some of the items carried for their customers.[41]

On 31st October, 1905, E G Williams & Co, of Bradford, instruct the Bennett Steamship Company to deliver one truss (weighing 86 pounds) of 75 yards of "Cheviotte Bleu" (value £4), and one truss (weighing 130 pounds) of 101 yards of fabric (value £5). The instruction is to "ship the goods by first steamer" and forward them to Lemy Père & fils, Brussels. These goods were possibly woollen cloth produced in the mills of Bradford. Another mill owner also using the services of the Bennett Steamship Company is Joseph Sykes & Co Ltd., of Rock Mills, Brockholes, near Huddersfield. Two copies of shipping instructions show the following. On the 1st November, 1905, the consignment of one truss of Worsted

Cloth, containing 44³/₄ yards to the value of £17 18s od, is to be shipped to Auguste Pick & Co of Leipzig. This mill no doubt is a regular customer of Bennetts, as there is evidence of another consignment instruction made two months later, again for one truss of Worsted Cloth, 49¹/₂ yards to the value of £59 10s 5d. The destination is also Auguste Pick & Co, Leipzig.

Bennetts also ship goods for Doulton & Company Limited of Burslem, "Potters To His Majesty The King". On 27th November 1905, truck number 143913 of the Midland Railway, delivers 161 pieces of Sanitary Earthenware to the dockside at Goole for shipment to Sanitas, Fredricksholms Kanal, Copenhagen *figure 101*. Hopefully lots of packing protected the earthenware just in case the passage turned out to be rough. Bennetts confirmed the shipment two days later with the addition of the phrase "at owner's risk". They amend the amount to 159 pieces, so presumably there was a discrepancy in the quantity, or this was due to damage. The shipping notice shows that Bennetts appear to act as agent in this delivery, since the order states "P.Pro Bennett Steamship Company Ltd" and the vessel they use is the ss Colne (owned by the Goole Steam Shipping Company Ltd.) bound for Copenhagen.

The following month on the 18th December, John Tullis & Son Limited, Tanners and Curriers, of St. Ann's Leather Works in Glasgow, make another shipping instruction. This was to ship one truss of "leather pickers", weighing 252 pounds with a value of £18. They requested that these were forwarded "under insurance" to Mr C Millard, Ghent, for F Christy of Lille. In January 1906, two shipments of printed cotton handkerchiefs leave Goole. One shipment despatched by Bennetts on the steamship Lisette, a collier owned by the Goole & West Riding Steam Ship Company Ltd. Messrs Th. De Bruycker, Brussels is the recipient of this cargo. The second via the steamship Derwent under Captain Arnold, bound for Hamburg, to Messrs Emden Sohne of Hamburg, on

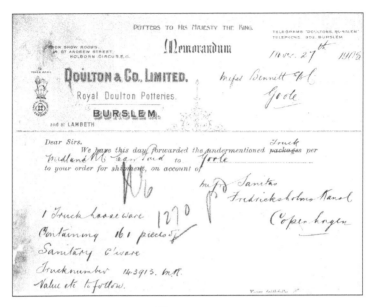

Figure 101

the 17th January. This second consignment had originated from Ernest R Boon & Co of Belfast on the 12th January. They sent the case of 100 dozen (1200) handkerchiefs via the Fleetwood Steam Ship Company and instructed it be forwarded immediately to Mr Julius Rudert of Hamburg. He was perhaps the end customer, with Messrs Sohne, being an agent in Hamburg. These represent just a few examples of the various cargoes carried.

In contrast to these relatively 'light' goods is a cargo of considerable proportions. The photograph *figure 102* shows the Africa in the process of loading steam locomotives. Over several voyages in July and August 1906, the Africa transported 50 surplus Midland railway locomotives from Goole to Boulogne, for onward delivery to the Italian State Railways at Milan. This load could not be more diverse than the cargo of printed cotton handkerchiefs. The advertisement in *figure 103* shows that the Hydra, China and India no longer appear in the list of vessels. The Hydra, as mentioned previously, became the Stettin around 1895/6. Prior to 1905, the India transferred to J H Bennett of Penzance, Colliery Agents, Shipowners and Brokers. Apparently the China becomes the 'Georg' [George] in 1890, but evidence of this has not so far been uncovered. This advertisement from 1907 also shows the office address at 120 Rue Lafayette, Paris.

Figure 102

Business is booming for the Bennett Steamship Company and in 1908 new offices built to accommodate their London operations. Designed by English architect Stanley Davenport Adshead, the building reflects a sophisticated Georgian-revival style. The building, christened Denmark House, still stands at 15 Tooley Street, London, having survived the pounding to the city of London during the Second World War. Granted a Grade II listing on 1st July 1983, the official description of Denmark House reads as follows:

"Roof parapeted. 5 storeys with one-window range to Tooley Street and 3-window range to triangular plaza on return. Entrance to party wall under elaborate cartouche. Squat stone

1907 GOOLE TIMES ILLUSTRATED ALMANACK. 137

Bennett's Red Cross Line of Steamers.

REGULAR STEAM COMMUNICATION

BETWEEN

GOOLE AND BOULOGNE.

The powerful Screw Steamers AFRICA, MOPSA, SYRIA, BURMA, COREA, MALTA, or other Steamers will be despatched (weather permitting) as follows:—

GOOLE to BOULOGNE every WEDNESDAY, THURSDAY, and SATURDAY; returning every MONDAY, WEDNESDAY, and SATURDAY.

The Steamers ply in connection with the Lancashire and Yorkshire Railway Company, who run their trains alongside the Steamers at Goole, from which the Merchandise is transhipped direct, without the risk or expense of cartage. This is of great importance to Shippers, as it ensures a quick delivery of their Goods in a clean and undamaged condition.

Goods are carried at THROUGH RATES from all parts of the UNITED KINGDOM to all Towns in FRANCE, ITALY, GERMANY, BELGIUM, SWITZERLAND, &c., and must be specially addressed to the BENNETT STEAMSHIP COMPANY, LIMITED, GOOLE DOCKS (SOUTH SECTION), GOOLE.

Passenger Fares:—10s., Single; 17s. 6d., Return. Good accommodation.

For Rates and other information apply to the Owners,

BENNETT STEAMSHIP COMPANY, LIMITED.

Offices—Bank Chambers, Goole. 11, Nelson Street, Hull.
15, Tooley Street, London. 120, Rue Lafayette, Paris.
Quai Maritime, Boulogne-sur-Mer,
or to the Lancashire & Yorkshire Railway Company's Agents.

Telegrams—"Bennett, Goole." "Bennett, Bolougne-sur-Mer." "Steamship, Paris." "Cargo, Hull." "Cargaison, London."

Telephone—Goole, No. 7. Hull, No. 357. London, No. 353 Hop. Paris, No. 425-79.

Also Steamers **London & Boulogne** three times a week each way.

Figure 103

pilasters to ground-floor plate-glass windows. Upper-floor windows paired sashes, those to 3rd floor with shallow balcony enclosed by metal railings and floating cornices; stylized swags flank each window pair. Top storey with panels in contrasting colour; pedimented dormers. Above the cornice, in centre of long return, an elaborate carved plaque crested by a steamship and held in place by a pair of putti."[42]

A photograph of the building can be seen in *figure 104*. The photo tint *figure 105* by James Akerman of 8 Queen Square, London shows what the completed building would have looked like when first built. The small portico-fronted building to the left of the image either did not exist or has since been demolished as it is not standing today.

Figure 104

147

Figure 105

148

In 1908, on the day before Bank Holiday, dock workers load 67,000 packages of vegetables on to the three ships which leave France between 3pm and midnight to catch the Covent Garden market the next morning. Albert Chatelle writes:

"It was a day's record that was talked about for a very long time, but there were not only the packages of prunes, velvety peaches and chubby melons, golden grapes and fresh blossomed roses there were at times some more voluminous parcels which put to the test the strong arms of the Bennett teams and also those arms, even more strong, of the cranes spaced out on the Bennett Quay."

In this year, the sight of an even more unusual cargo must have caused some amusement. This attracted many crowds watching the delicate task of loading and unloading. Albert Chatelle writes of this story:

"It is thus that one saw in 1908 embarking for London in the presence of a crowd of curious people of the Caravanage of Bostock Circus, then one of the most important in Europe. The putting on board of the animals on this improvised Noah's Ark gave rise at times to some amusing instances. I remember having seen an Elephant take delicately in his trunk a man on the Quay and drop him overboard when the Bennett workmen hastened to fish out of the water this new specie of Jonah."

Figures 106 & 107 are photographs of the Bostock Circus.

The photograph *figure 108* shows Herbert Thomas Bennett and his wife (both seated) together with some of their children and grandchildren taken circa 1910.

Figure 109 is a photograph from about 1913 showing the Syria and another Bennett vessel in Goole Docks.

Figure 106

Figure 107

Figure 108

Figure 109

151

Chapter 7
Troubled Times

Sometime around or just before 1914, the Bennett jetty just down river from the port of Goole ceases to be used by the Bennett Steamship Company, when the Goole Shipbuilding & Repairing Company obtains a lease on the site from the Aire & Calder Navigation Company. Shipbuilding berths subsequently occupy this area. Also, in 1913, the Bennett Steamship Company moves its French operations from the first floor of the harbour station, to the new dock opened at this time, 'Bassin Loubet'. The first ship to enter on a Monday morning in October 1913 is one belonging to the Bennett Steamship Company.

In the summer of 1914, one of Bennetts' ships has a serious collision that thankfully does not result in the loss of life. For those on board at the time, however, it must have been a truly frightening experience. The passengers included two grandsons of the late John Bennett. The Goole Times reports the account on Friday 17th July 1914:

COLLISION AT SEA
S.S. BURMA, OF GOOLE SERIOUSLY DAMAGED
EXCITING SCENES
GOOLE LADY'S STORY OF HER EXPERIENCES

"On Friday, the ss Burma, of Goole, had a narrow escape from being sunk in the North Sea. Besides her crew of sixteen, she had on board six passengers, including Miss Watkins, the captain's daughter, Miss Brennand, daughter of Councillor W. Brennand, Goole, two boys, sons of Mr Herbert Bennett, of Potter Grange, a gentleman residing at Folkestone, and a lady residing at Barnby Dun.

The Burma, which is owned by the Bennett Steamship Company, of Goole and London, left Goole with a general cargo. After leaving the River Humber behind she encountered dense fog. The vessel had proceeded on her journey about twenty miles, when, without the slightest warning, she collided with the s.s. Staveley, a passenger steamer, owned by the Great Central Railway Company, returning from the Continent to Grimsby.

The Burma had her syren [sic] going practically the whole of the time, and that of another vessel could be heard. Suddenly the bow of the Staveley was seen to loom out of the fog. She was only a dozen yards away from the Burma, and before anything could be done to avert the collision, the Staveley had crashed into the bows of the Goole vessel. The impact was tremendous. The Burma went heeling over to port.

Captain Watkins, master of the Burma, the mate, Mr Prentice, and others were on the bridge at the time, and while considerable alarm was felt there was not the least sign of panic, and crew and passengers acted with commendable pluck and coolness.

It was at once realised the Burma was in a serious predicament. Captain Watkins and others with him on the bridge were hurled against the rails of the bridge with considerable force, and the captain sustained some injury to his shoulder. Immediately the vessels collided, Captain Watkins got into communication with the captain of the Staveley, and asked him if he could take his passengers on board his vessel. He replied that his ship seemed to be as badly damaged as the Goole ship, but that he would stand by and do all he could. The officers on the Burma reported that the vessel was sinking, and Captain Watkins ordered the lifeboats out. The crew went to work in businesslike manner, and in quick time one of the lifeboats was successfully launched, and all the passengers were safely placed in the boat. While the boat was being launched the passengers were all provided with a lifebelt each, which was fastened around their bodies. The sea was not very rough, it was only choppy, and thus the efforts of the crew were not unduly hampered. The mate and three sailors manned the boat, which was taken some distance away from the two vessels lying close to each other. Eventually Mr Prentice, carrying out an order from the captain, returned to the Burma and made a close examination of the damage done, and he reported that the ship could make for port with comparative safety. The captain of the Staveley again inquired if he could make any service, but was informed that he could not. The passengers were removed from the lifeboat to the ship again, and soon after the Burma began to steam slowly back to Hull, reaching the third port on Friday night.

Mr. J Bentley Bennett, managing director of the company, was informed of what had taken place by wire, and he immediately went to Hull to look at the vessel. After an examination it was found that the vessel could make the journey to Goole, which she did with her own steam, but was accompanied by a tug brought to help her to swing round in the river.

The Staveley went on her way to Grimsby, where she also arrived safely on Friday. The Burma was in a pitiable plight, her stern being knocked in and her plates being bulged.

Her cargo was transferred into the ss Calder, which has been chartered from the Lancashire and Yorkshire Railway (Goole Steam Shipping) Co, and which will run in the Boulogne service until the damage to the Burma is repaired.

R. Hudson, first mate on the Staveley, it is interesting to note is a Goole man, and was at one time captain of the Burma.

Miss Brennand was one of the passengers, and on her way to Paris, to spend a holiday. After they got to sea, she told a 'Journal' reporter, they ran into thick fog. The Burma's syren [sic] was kept almost continually blowing, she said. Nothing could be seen through the darkness prevailing, and no sounds were to be heard except the noise of the sea and of the ship's engines, and occasionally faint sounds from the syrens [sic] of other ships. She was on the bridge with Captain Watkins, Miss Watkins, and the mate. Suddenly she saw a ship's head loom out of the fog. "It was coming straight for us at full speed, and was not more than a dozen yards or so from us. I cast a glance at the captain and I could tell by his face that he had also seen the vessel and realised the danger we were in. At this time the Burma's syren [sic] was going. Much sooner than I can tell it, there was a loud crash and the grinding of steel upon steel sounded horrible. Our ship seemed to jump in the air and then come down to its side. I instinctively clutched at the rails and probably this saved me from injury. The captain, I noticed, was hurled against the rails, and he sustained an injury to the shoulder, though I don't think it is very serious. Anyhow, he continued to do his work and gave orders. I heard the mate say the vessel was going down, and I heard Capt. Watkins shout orders for the lifeboats to be launched. While this was being done I went below to the cabin for a few things, and then I heard the two boys, John and Tom Bennell, aged about 9 and 10 respectively, crying. They had heard the noise of the collision and had felt the ship tremble from end to end. They asked if the boat was sinking, I told them it was not, but honestly I thought it was." Asked what were her feelings at the time, Miss Brennand said she did not feel unduly dismayed for some inexplicable reason, and she tried to comfort the two boys by talking to them and generally looking after them. She brought the boys up on deck and then she noticed the Staveley's decks crowded with passengers, but there was no panic on either vessel. In the meantime a lifeboat had been launched, and Miss Brennand said she was

155

bodily lifted over the boat side and dropped into the arms of another sailor and then put in the lifeboat.

We were in the lifeboat for close upon half an hour, a little away from the two ships, and then the mate, Mr Prentice, on order from the captain, came near to the Burma to examine her damage more closely. He found that her bows had been fearfully battered in, but that she was not making water, and this he reported to the captain. Capt. Watkins then decided that he would return to Hull.

The passengers in the lifeboat were now to be transferred back to the ship, and this proved an even more difficult matter than getting from the ship to the lifeboat. A rope ladder was put out, but there being a big swell on, the boat rocked, and it was difficult to gain the rope."

Fortunately this collision happens in peace time, and the ship and her occupants survive. Later that same year, however, a time of fear and uncertainty begins at 11pm on 4th August 1914, in the shape of World War I. Two days later on the 6th, the destroyer 'Lark', along with her sister destroyers 'Lance', 'Laurel', and 'Linnet', all acting under the command of Captain Fox on board the doomed 'Amphion', chase and sink the German mine-layer Königin Luise. The crew from the destroyers helps to save the survivors of the Amphion when she collides with German floating mines. The First Lord of the Admiralty speaks in the House of Commons two days after the disaster condemning the destructive nature of these mines scattered randomly around the seas. He points out that they destroy not only enemy vessels and warships but innocent merchant vessels and their crews going about their everyday business. This fact would impact frightfully close to home for the Bennett Steamship Company, as this period in the story demonstrates.

At the outbreak of war a mutual system of insurance covered four-fifths of British shipping. This provided an indemnity for war risks incurred by ships at sea at the outbreak of war, up to the time they reached the nearest British or neutral port. The insurance rates for covering actual war risks then leapt to thoroughly prohibitive figures. The result of this was to close down several routes entirely for a brief period, since voyages could only be undertaken at significant financial loss. On the day that war breaks out Lloyd George announces in the House of Commons the introduction of a special scheme of state insurance for shipping. The purpose of this was to encourage ships to remain at sea and maintain trade. The government would fix the premiums and receive 80% of them assuming responsibility for 80% of the risk. The remaining risk would be covered with the insurance companies and combinations. The government also opened an office for the state insurance of cargoes, reserving the right to alter the premiums. The Bennett family would have been carefully noting all these details relating to insurance of their vessels.

Mary Eleanor Bennett marries William Robert George King Ormsby on the 4th January 1915 at Kingston-Upon-Thames. Tragically, on the 22nd April 1915, Lance Corporal William Ormsby, of the Canadian Infantry (Eastern Ontario Regiment) 8407, 2nd Battalion, is killed in action. Mary goes on to become a paediatrician at Great Ormond Street Hospital. She dies 14th August 1962.

The British Admiralty used the Africa, Mopsa, and Syria for the war effort. The Mopsa, however, would return to civilian service and transport cars to Boulogne for the British Red Cross.

For the Bennett Steamship Company, this war claimed its first casualty on Thursday 16th September 1915 whilst the Africa was sailing from London having been on Admiralty service. The report of this incident appears in the Goole Times of Friday 24th September 1915:

GOOLE SAILORS TERRIBLE DEATH
THE FIRE-HOLE OF THE SS AFRICA
HOW THE BODY WAS FOUND

"In connection with the beaching of the ss Africa of Messrs. Bennett & Co., which was reported in Saturday's Goole Journal, a tragedy has been brought to light, in which was involved the death of a Goole man, Charles Henry Pettican.

The vessel had left London on Thursday morning, and after she had met with disaster, Pettican was found standing in the fire-hole. His foot and knee had been caught in the wreckage of the engine room, and he had been unable to extricate himself. The water had risen only a fraction of an inch above his mouth and nose, but it is believed that death was due to shock, and that he was spared the agony of a lingering death with the water slowly creeping higher and higher above his mouth. Pettican was 47 years of age, and leaves a widow and eight children, five of whom are quite young.

Pettican had been in the service of the Bennett Steamship Co. for twenty years, and had been on the Africa for twelve years, having been one of the crew which brought the vessel to Goole when she was built.

Another member of the crew, also a fireman who hailed from Gravesend, is missing but the captain, officers, and the rest of the crew are safe. The ss Africa, which had been on Admiralty service, will, it is thought, be salved.

THE FUNERAL
VICAR'S ELOQUENT TRIBUTE TO SEAMEN

Impressive to a degree were the last funeral rites, which were solemnised on Tuesday afternoon at the Goole cemetery.

The cortege which left the house was headed by a number of late shipmates and friends of the deceased, and included: Mr. A. Lockwood (stevedore of Bennett Steamship Co.), whilst representing the company there were also Messrs. E. Ellis,

G.W. Dunham, J.T. Haigh, R. Hodgson (a friend and shipmate for years), and S. Danielson (cook on the ss.Africa), with Messrs. A. Hall and W.J. Perritt (National Sailors' and Firemen's Union), Mr. E. Petman (Shipping Federation, Ltd., and the Crown Inn Sick and Dividing Club), Mr. Meggitt (friend), Messrs. R. Shaw, J. Champion, J.N. Crabtree, T. Flower, A. Coy, and H. Dupres (National Sailors' and Firemen's Union), W. Coates, W. Carroll, J. Blackwell, and S.C. Smith (Royal Naval Reserve, and in uniform), T. Knott, J. Dickinson, G. Ferry, and W. Perritt, (National Sailors' and Firemen's Union), Charles Proctor (Ouse Street), John Macintosh, Wm Tasker, and Richard Raywood (friends), with Mr. J.T. Pierson, undertaker, North Street."

The account lists family mourners and representatives of the company, and then carries on listing tributes, some of which can be seen below:

"Among many beautiful floral tributes were: - "In affectionate remembrance, from his sorrowing wife and family", "In loving memory from father, mother and sisters"....... "In loving memory, Sam and Ada"......... "With sincere sympathy; The Directors and Staff Bennetts S.S. Co.", "With sincere regret and deepest sympathy Capt. and Officers s.s. Africa"....."

"After the burial service had been read in the Cemetery Church, the Vicar of Goole speaking with evident emotion to the mourners said: – "Surely at a time like this, when so many hearts are anxious and so many homes have the figure of death hanging over them, it is well to fix our thoughts upon the words of our Lord. And as we lay our dead hero friend in his last sleeping place, let us remember that though his body is laid in the grave his soul has gone back to God, who gave it. Whilst it is true that every Christian man and woman ought to rejoice in the fact that Jesus Christ has overcome death yet at the same time one realises how deep is the sorrow of those who have to pass through the vale of affliction, and so we give you our deepest sympathy. The sympathy of the town goes out to you, and it is left to me to voice it, and I do so with the deepest and sincerest of sympathy. It is indeed a deep joy to know that Charles Henry Pettican was a model husband and a good father. I speak what I know. It is a joy to me to know he was one of the very best of workmen, loyal and true to the firm he served so well and so long. It must be a deep joy to his dear ones to know that as his death had to come it found him at the post of duty. When this war is over the greatest praise will be given to the men in our merchant service – and they deserve it. These men, who, in spite of unparalleled dangers have gone on doing their duty. The English sailor of the merchant service is one of the finest men in God's world, and when a man has met his death at the post of duty we thank God for his noble example: and we know that such a man is welcomed by Christ. He (deceased) died at the post of duty. He did his duty to his King and country. He is one of the noble army of sailors who have died doing their duty, and whilst we give your our deepest sympathy, we are proud to think he died doing his duty. And so we leave him 'Safe in the arms of Jesus, safe on the Saviour's breast'. He who loved sailors so deeply, that he wanted to find disciples found them in the ranks of the sailors, has still the same heart of love for His sailors to-day, and Christ has greeted him safe on the other shore."

Personal tragedy also strikes the Bennett family when George Spilman Bennett Todd, grandson of the late John Bennett, becomes a victim of the war. The second eldest son of Mary Adelaide and her husband Daniel Hewitt Todd, he dies on the 24th March, 1916, near Vermelles in France at the young age of just 18 years.

Three months later, tragedy comes again to a vessel of the Bennett Steamship Company. It was the Burma which survived the collision with the Staveley in 1914. The Burma arrives in Goole on the 10th June 1916 under Captain Goodworth carrying ballast from London. Arriving on the same day is the Malta under Captain Watkins with a general cargo from Boulogne. Some time after the 11th June the Burma leaves Goole. She is under Captain Goodworth when disaster strikes the vessel off the English Coast 5 miles north-east of the Shipwash Light vessel. The Goole Times Friday 30th June 1916 gives a full account:

LOSS OF THE SS BURMA
MINED IN THE NORTH SEA
SEVEN OF THE CREW KILLED

"News was received in Goole of the loss of the s.s. Burma, which was either mined or torpedoed in the North Sea off the English coast on Friday and sank. Of those on board, nine were saved, including the master, the first and second mates, and the second engineer. Seven of the crew lost their lives, being either killed or drowned.

Included in the list of the lost was Mr. J. Shay, the chief engineer.

SAVED

Those saved were : -

Capt. Goodworth
First Officer Greenwood
Second Officer Eccles
Second Engineer Bradford
Gates
Rorrison
Taylor
Kirby
Vause

MISSING

The full list of missing is as follows: -

Mr. Shay
Champion
Duffield
Jackson
Dudding
Gilyon
Turner

161

The Burma was a steel screw steamer of 724 tons gross, and 693 tons net register. She was built in 1891 by Messrs. Austins, of Sunderland, and was engined by Messrs. Clark, of Sunderland. She was built for the Bennett Steamship Company, Limited, and has been in the Goole and Boulogne and the London and Boulogne trade. She was last in Goole on June 11th.

Mr. J. Bentley Bennett, the Managing Director of the Line, in an interview with a "Journal" reporter wished it to be known how deeply he and the firm deplore the loss of the men, especially of Mr. Shay, who was a very old and respected servant of the company, and their senior engineer. Of Mr. Shay, it is somewhat pathetic to recall that he was serving on the s.s. Africa another steamer of the Bennett Line which was lost last year from a similar cause and was only prevented by illness from sailing on her last and ill-fated voyage.

Mr. Shay, the chief engineer, lived at Broadway, and is survived by a wife and three children.

Several of the lost sailors have left widows and families of small children.

RESCUE BY THE S.S. F.STOBART
CAPT. STUART'S THRILLING STORY

How the Burma came by her fate was made clear when the s.s. F. Stobart reached Goole on Saturday. In an interview with a representative of the "Goole Journal", Capt. Stuart said that the catastrophe occurred about 6-30pm. The weather was fine, and the F. Stobart was following about 60 or 80 yards behind the Burma, when suddenly there was a terrific explosion under the fore part of the latter, which lifted the foremast clean out of the deck, and flung it over the bridge and the after part of the ship. The force of the explosion was so great that it shook the F. Stobart from stem to stern. The F. Stobart at once proceeded to the rescue, and when she reached the wrecked vessel she found three men in a boat which had been launched, and four others with lifebelts on struggling in the water. She took these on board, and then took off the steward who for some reason had been left behind when the boat put off. The explosion had completely wrecked the fore part of the ship, and the six men who were in the forecastle, no doubt enjoying a period of relaxation after tea, must have been killed instantaneously. The captain and mate were slightly injured by the falling mast. When the steward was being got off the vessel he was asked if there were any more aboard, and relayed that there was only the chief engineer, who was lying across the winch dead. It is probable, Capt. Stuart thought, that he had been struck by the mast or something dislodged by it. When the F. Stobart reached the Burma, said Capt. Stuart, the forepart of the vessel was down, the water being level with the lower part of the bridge, the stern was high out of the sea, and the propeller raced until something in the machinery gave way, and it ceased to revolve.

The men of the Burma were in a dazed condition when taken on board, and the crew of the F. Stobart were doing their best to make them comfortable, when a torpedo boat came on the scene and took the survivors off with a view to landing them at Harwich, whence they reached Goole by train.
Capt. Stuart had no doubt whatever that the cause of the disaster was a mine, and he relates that about three months ago he had a similar experience near the same place in rescuing the crew of the Harriet, a Danish vessel.

When the F. Stobart last saw the Burma she was still afloat.

ENGINEER'S HEROISM

A stirring story of heroism arising out of the sinking of the s.s. Burma has come to light. It appears that when the vessel was seen to be sinking, and the crew were leaving in the lifeboats, one of the men gave the alarm that the discharge from the engines was filling the boats. There were then left on board but the second mate, Mr. Eccles, Riddings Farm, Airmyn, the

2nd engineer Mr. Branford, 44 Dunhill Road, Goole, and the steward, Amos Gates.

Without hesitation the engineer gave up his prospect of immediate rescue, and taking his life in his hands, went below to turn off the steam. The vessel was sinking at the time. Her head on the starboard side was blown clean off and had she kept "way" on her, she must have gone straight down, and the boats, with the men in them, would have been drawn under by the suction. His task accomplished the engineer found on his return to deck that the last boat had put off, and that he, together with the 2nd mate and the steward, had been left behind. The second mate cried out; "Jump for it, Herbert", and Mr. Branford sprang into the water. All three were eventually rescued and taken on board the s.s. F. Stobart.

Mr. Branford's action in going right down into the engine room, under such conditions – the propeller "racing" out of the water, and with every prospect of the steamer sinking while he was below – required the courage of a hero."

The F Stobart arrives back in Goole on June 24th the day after the tragedy of the Burma. Two other Bennett vessels also arrive in Goole on that day, the Malta under Captain Watkins, and Mopsa under Captain Greenwood.

Only three weeks later, tragedy strikes again. The Mopsa hits a mine in the North Sea 7 miles south of Lowestoft however, thankfully, rescuers save the entire crew. Captain Greenwood had been in charge of the Mopsa; the same captain in charge of the Africa when tragedy struck that vessel. The following account appears in The Goole Times, Friday 21st July 1916:

ANOTHER GOOLE VESSEL LOST
S.S. MOPSA MINED IN THE NORTH SEA
WHOLE OF THE CREW SAFE

"News reached Goole on Sunday that the s.s. Mopsa, belonging to the Bennett Steamship Co. Ltd., had been sunk about 4.30 that morning through striking a mine in the North Sea, but that happily the whole of the crew had been saved and landed at Lowestoft. The vessel was in charge of Capt. Greenwood, the senior captain of the company, who was also the master of the s.s. Africa, belonging to the same company, which was sunk about twelve months ago. Messrs. Bennett have thus had the misfortune to lose three of their fleet, the Burma being mined on June 23rd, with the loss of seven lives.

The Mopsa which was built at Glasgow in 1902 was 225ft in length, with 33-1 beam and 33-5 depth of hold, Her gross tonnage is 885, net 385 tons. The three vessels which have been lost had for many years carried on the regular trade of the company between Goole and Boulogne the other vessels of the fleet being engaged in the London-Boulogne trade.

The Mopsa left Goole on Saturday morning for Boulogne with a full general cargo, which included a large quantity of agriculture implements, which were carried on deck. An attempt was made to beach the vessel after the explosion but it was unsuccessful, and she now lies sunk off the coast. It appears that when the Mopsa was mined a large Newcastle steamer went to her assistance, and was helping her towards the shore, when she herself was struck by a mine and sank, all the crew being picked up. The Mopsa now lies off the Essex coast on her side in a considerable depth of water, and there is little hope of raising her. Her cargo was valued at £60,000."

Seven months later, yet another ship falls victim to the war. The company lose one of their flagship vessels the Malta as recounted in The Goole Times on 23rd February 1917:

THE LOSS OF THE MALTA
SANK IN TWENTY MINUTES
CREW'S UNPLEASANT EXPERIENCE

"Further particulars are to hand in reference to the loss of the s.s. Malta, belonging to the Bennett Steamship Co., Ltd.,

Goole, which, as briefly reported in the "Goole Times" was sunk through collision with another vessel last week.

It appears that the accident occurred in the early hours of the morning. The vessel that ran into her was a Japanese ship. The Malta was struck near the engine room, but it was impossible, owing to the wreckage, to make an investigation of the damage. The vessel began to sink and the crew, numbering 15, at once took to the boats. Naturally, at that hour, they were in various stages of dishabille, several were clad only in shirt and trousers and many were without boots or hats. The weather was very severe, and during the hour and a half or so that elapsed before they were picked up by a British torpedo boat, however, they were well looked after, and later in the day they were able to return home to Goole, little the worse for their terrible adventure except the chief engineer, Mr. Miller, who is still suffering from exposure, and Capt. Watkins, who is recovering from an injury to his knee sustained in climbing up the side of the torpedo boat. The crew unfortunately lost all their belongings. The Malta sank in 15 to 20 minutes after the impact."

The Japanese steamer that hits the Malta is the "Kadjee Maru" and the collision occurs in fog. Captain William Watkins previously served on the Mopsa and Burma.

During this war, Edith and Ingham Spinks move their family down to Rugby in 1917, whilst retaining their house at Pateley Bridge in Nidderdale.

In the course of the next twelve months, two more of the late John Bennett's grandsons fall victim to the war. Robert Granville Bennett, son of Herbert Thomas Bennett, killed in action and buried 4th October 1917 at Polycon Wood. The following year on the 28th August 1918, Mary Adelaide loses yet another child, her eldest son (who also had a twin sister) Gordon Hewitt Todd aged 22, near Etaples, France. It is also believed that Albert Edmund Bennett dies sometime between 1914 and 1918.

The Great War hits the Bennett family hard in many ways, as indeed it affected countless other families. In addition to the personal tragedies, they lost in total four vessels; what a tremendous impact this must have had on the company. It is quite touching to learn of a discussion held on an afternoon at the end of December 1918 between John Bentley Bennett and Monsieur Georges Honoré. The Boulogne Review of 8th February 1927 recounts this as follows:

"I am reminded always of the afternoon at the end of December 1918, where in our small war office on Rue du Pot d'Etain, we remained for more than four hours, my old and faithful friend Mr. Bentley Bennett and me, to examine all sides of the position that was excessively difficult. The decision taken then was the start of the revival for the Bennett Company."

After the end of this war, the company does indeed begin to rebuild its fleet, as the next chapter shows.

Chapter 8
Peacetime Again

On Monday 6th November 1899 (20 years earlier), a vessel christened the Gresham was launched. Built by Taylor and Mitchell of Greenock (yard no 3), and owned by John White of London, she weighed 708 gross tons. This vessel had an unsettled life, and after only one month, transferred to the New Zealand Shipping Company becoming the Petone in 1900. The following photograph *figure 110* shows the Petone some time prior to 1921 probably in South Wales. The small boat Kyles (in front of the Petone) now lies preserved in the Scottish Maritime Museum at Glasgow.

Figure 110

The following list shows the previous owners of the vessel:

1900 - New Zealand Shipping Company.
1903 - Blackball Coal Company, London.
1910 - Canterbury Steam Shipping, Lyttleton.
1916 - Todhunter & Montgomery, Lyttleton.
1916 - Cuningham, Shaw & Co, London.
1917 - Petone Shipping Company, Cardiff.
1920 - Zenith Steam Shipping Company, Cardiff.

In a voyage from Blyth to Rouen on 8th October 1921, the Petone becomes grounded 4 miles east of the French coastal town of Fecamp. Refloated the following day, 9th October, Bennetts purchase the Petone and immediately rename her Sparta. Captain William White is the master of the ss Sparta, until his death, when Captain Charles Willmott takes over the command. The photograph *figure 111* shows the Sparta in dock.

Lloyds register 1920-1, lists the owners of the Petone as the Zenith Steam Shipping Co. Ltd. (Loan Williams & Co), and her registered port London. Her change of ownership to the Bennett Steamship Company appears in the supplement to this register. The specification and her new name can be seen in *figure 112*.

In early 1921, there is also the celebration of the 25-year jubilee for one of the loyal Bennett employees, Monsieur Georges Honoré. Having joined the company in 1896 working on the Boulogne operation, he is at this point in the story a director alongside John Bentley Bennett. A Monsieur Duriez, speaking on the occasion of the jubilee, pays a fitting tribute to Monsieur Honoré: "You were always for us the good boss, one who does not consider his assistants his subordinates, but treats as friends, who would never take your name in vain. It is the secret of the affection for you, employees and workers, proud to work under your skillful direction." Boulogne Review 8th February 1927.

Figure 111

Figure 112

Ship No	112654
Name	Sparta (ex Petone, ex Gresham)
Description	Steel Screw
Master	Captain William White
Tonnage	Gross 708, Under deck 503, net 388
Dimensions	Length – 185.4 Breadth – 29.2 Depth – 11.8
Engines	T3Cy15", 25" & 40"-27" 160lb 70lb 82RHP 1SB, 3pf, GS56, HS1490 McKie & Baxter, Glasgow
Builder	Taylor & Mitchell, Greenock
Built	1900
Owner	Bennett Steam Ship Co Ltd
Registered port	Goole
Port of survey	GMS [believed to be Grimsby]
Class	100 A1 (built under special survey)

In recognition of his services Monsieur Georges Honoré receives a bronze statue by the sculptor Gauquié with an inscription – "Rien ne résiste à l'effort" - roughly translated, "Nothing withstand to the effort". They present his wife with an elegant basket of flowers.

Around 1921 John Bentley Bennett becomes the Manager of the Channel Steam Ship Company Limited. The only vessel listed to this company at this time is the steamship Whitgift most likely named after the village where John Bennett senior lies buried. Built in 1917 by Ardrossen Dry Dock and Shipbuilding Co. Ltd., and first named the 'Lillena', she later becomes 'Madame Lundi'. Her specification details (taken from Lloyds Register) are in *figure 113*.

Figure 113

Ship No	140523
Name	Whitgift (ex Madame Lundi, ex Lillena)
Description	Steel Screw
Master	
Tonnage	Gross 287, Under deck 203, net 104
Dimensions	Length – 120.1 Breadth – 23.6 Depth – 10.3
Engines	C2Cy.15.5" & 33"-24" 140lb 64 RHP 1SB 2pf, GS38, HS1209 Shields Eng Co Ltd S Shl
Builder	Ardrossan DD & SB Co Ltd Ardrossan
Built	1917
Owner	Channel Steam Ship Co Ltd (J Bentley Bennett Mgr)
Registered port	London
Port of survey	Goole
Class	100 A1

The Whitgift is only 5 years old when John Bennett junior acquires her. The registered office of the Channel Steam Ship Co. Ltd. is 15 Tooley Street (their London office). In the following year, however, the Channel Steam Ship Company moves to 109 Fenchurch Street, London, and the year after that to Ocean House, 24-5 Great Tower Street, London.

In what looks like an attempt to rebuild the Bennett Steam Ship Company another vessel joins the fleet in 1922/3. This is the Volga purchased from W H Bowater Ltd. Built back in 1881 for the Belfast Steam Shipping Company the original name of this ship is the Topic. During 1895 to 1905, this vessel belongs to the Volana Shipping Co. Ltd., 17 Water Street, Liverpool (Rogers & Bright). It then changed ownership to the Volga Steam Shipping Co. Ltd., one of the oldest steamship companies in Russia. The Volga engaged in the coasting trade and accommodated 27 seamen. Registered to Bennetts in Lloyds Register 1923/4, *figure 114* shows the specification. Captain John Fielder is the master of the Volga until he joins the Goole Pilotage Service. Captain Fred Whitehead then assumes command. Some of the crew at this time were mate Lee Voguer, second mate John Cooke, chief engineer William Leggott, steward John Lawson, and seamen Mr E Axup and Charles Sap.[43]

Figure 114

Ship No	83929
Name	Volga (ex Topic)
Description	Iron Screw Schooner
Master	
Tonnage	Gross 281, Under deck 238, net 101
Dimensions	Length – 155.3 Breadth – 21.7 Depth – 10.5
Engines	C2Cy 19.5" & 36"-27" 75lb 50 RHP 1SB, 2pf, GS30, HS1110 by M'Ilwaine & Lewis Belfast
Builder	M'Ilwaine & Lewis Belfast
Built	1881
Owner	Bennett Steam Ship Co Ltd
Registered port	Goole
Port of survey	
Class	100 A1 (built under special survey)

John Bentley Bennett starts trading briskly in stocks and shares from at least the 1920s to the 1940s through his broker William West and Sons, Bowlalley Lane, Hull.[44] Just some of the companies he invests in appear below.

Stock
Furness Withy & Company Limited
Beunos Aires Western Railway Limited
Quebec Central Railway Company
London & North Eastern Railway Company
Sheffield & South Yorkshire Navigation Company
Canadian Pacific Railway Company
Central Argentine Railway Limited
Manitoba
Hessle Gas Company
Aire & Calder Navigation Company

Shares
Nan Dyke Consolidated Mines Limited
Hudson Bay Company Limited
Goole House Property Company Limited
Humber Graving Docks & Engineering Company Limited
Reckitt & Sons Limited
Amalgamated Dental Company Limited
Unilever
Belgian National Railways
Brazilian Traction Light & Power Company
Bentleys Yorkshire Breweries
Camp Bird Limited
Spring Mines Limited
William France Fenwick & Company Limited
Shell Transport & Trading Company Limited
Mousse Mines Limited
Village Deep Limited
Imperial Tobacco Company Limited
General Steam Navigation Company Limited

Figure 115

The photograph *figure 115* shows John Bentley Bennett in 1926. This was also the year of The General Strike, when workers in key industries walked out. These workers included dock workers and this must have affected the Bennett Steamship Company operations. It was a busy time for the company since during this year they brought over 8000 Citreon and Renault motor vehicles into Britain to be used as London taxis. The following advertisements – *figure 116 & 117* from the Boulogne Review 1926, show firstly their London agent, Blackmores Motor Transport Limited who were importing Vauxhall vehicles through the Bennett company, and secondly a general company advertisement.

BLACKMORES

Motor Transport Co Ltd

LONDON

Camionneurs officiels de la Compagnie BENNETT

CAMIONNAGE RAPIDE
des DENRÉES PÉRISSABLES aux MARCHÉS de LONDRES

CAMIONS TOUJOURS en ATTENTE
POUR LES LIVRAISONS URGENTES

ORGANISATION SPÉCIALE
pour la MANUTENTION et le TRANSPORT des VOITURES
et CHASSIS AUTOMOBILES

Un personnel expérimenté et connaissant particulièrement les besoins du trafic français est mis à la disposition de la clientèle.

GARAGES ET ATELIERS :

VAUXHALL

LONDON

Pour les ordres de camionnage s'adresser :

VICTORIA WHARVES
LIME HOUSE
LONDON E.
AND
109, FENCHURCH STREET
LONDON, E. C. 3

Figure 116

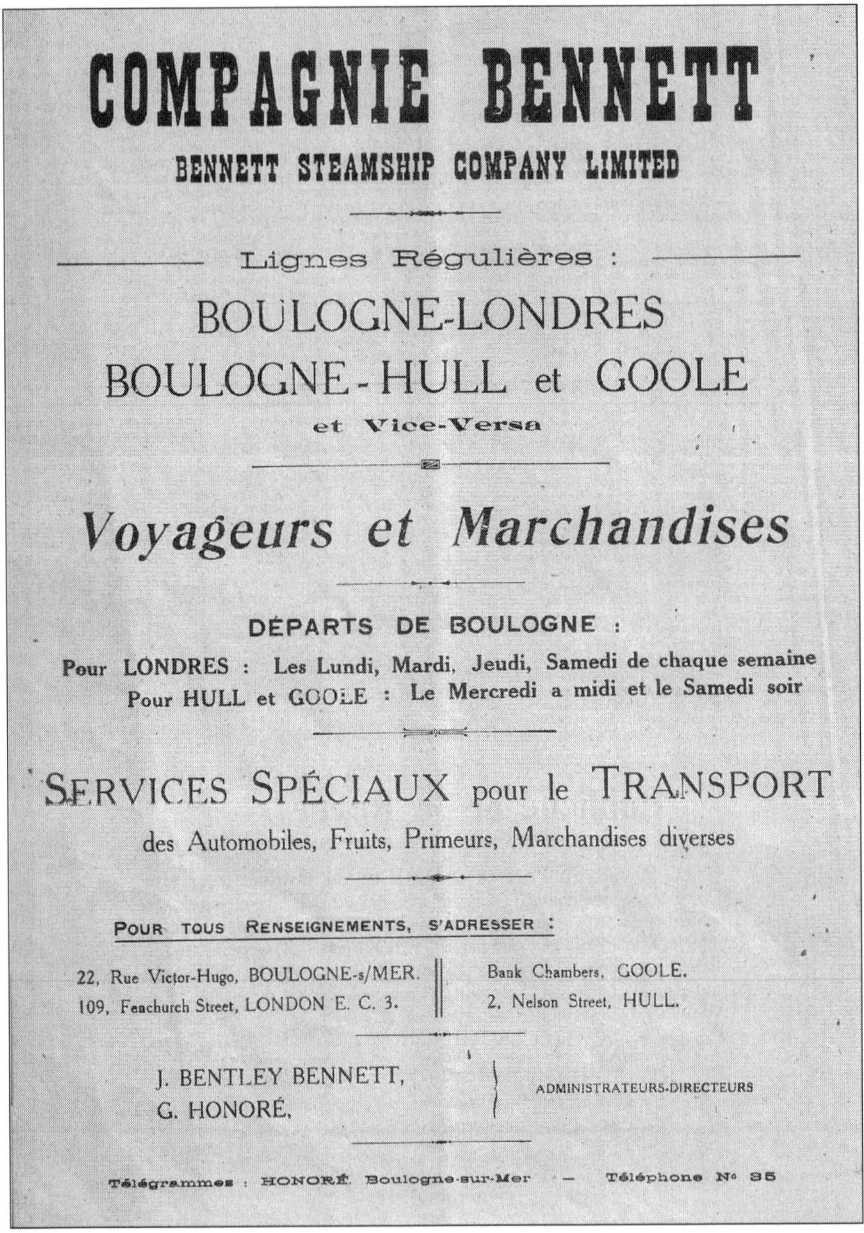

COMPAGNIE BENNETT

BENNETT STEAMSHIP COMPANY LIMITED

Lignes Régulières :

BOULOGNE-LONDRES

BOULOGNE-HULL et GOOLE

et Vice-Versa

Voyageurs et Marchandises

DÉPARTS DE BOULOGNE :

Pour LONDRES : Les Lundi, Mardi, Jeudi, Samedi de chaque semaine

Pour HULL et GOOLE : Le Mercredi a midi et le Samedi soir

SERVICES SPÉCIAUX pour le TRANSPORT

des Automobiles, Fruits, Primeurs, Marchandises diverses

POUR TOUS RENSEIGNEMENTS, S'ADRESSER :

22, Rue Victor-Hugo, BOULOGNE-s/MER.
109, Fenchurch Street, LONDON E. C. 3.

Bank Chambers, GOOLE.
2, Nelson Street, HULL.

J. BENTLEY BENNETT,
G. HONORÉ,
ADMINISTRATEURS-DIRECTEURS

Télégrammes : HONORÉ Boulogne-sur-Mer — Téléphone No 35

Figure 117

Also in the Boulogne Review of the same year, are details of the trade through Boulogne. At this time, the Bennett Steamship Company has a serious competitor operating to and from Boulogne – the Southern Railway Company. In the month of June 1926, Bennetts have 35 vessels arriving from London, and only 8 vessels arriving from Hull and Goole collectively. The departures were 34 and 11 vessels respectively. Their competitor, the Southern Railway Company, has significantly higher numbers with 69 vessels arriving from Folkestone, and 68 departing from Boulogne to Folkestone. Import tonnage decreased from the previous month, but export tonnage remained strong in excess of 17,000 tons. Approximately 900 tons of this is in cars and spare parts, with 11,000 tons in fruit and vegetables (in the main blueberries from Alsace and cherries from Boulogne). Despite many of the cherry harvests affected by the presence of a fly in the fruit, export continued with edible fruit bearing a certificate of quality. In addition to the main commodities exported, 424 tons of chocolate, 384 tons of cheese, and 711 tons of wine also left Boulogne. The review stated that exports of flowers, poultry, wool and iron were on the decrease.

In 1926, Herbert Thomas Bennett moves from Potter Grange to "Hafodty" (now known as Edgerton House) on Loughborough Road, Ruddington near Nottingham. The move was necessary since the owner of Potter Grange, Baron Wittenham CB, decides to sell at auction on the 21st January 1925.[45] He then serves notice on his tenants, Herbert Thomas Bennett and The Goole Urban District Council, to leave. The sale catalogue describes the Grange as a 'Capital Residence' with entrance hall, dining, drawing and breakfast rooms, billiard room, office, kitchen, four dairies, three principal bedrooms, nursery, two servant bedrooms, attic, bathroom, toilet and out offices. In the grounds are large stables, saddle rooms, barns, sheds, piggeries, foreman's cottage, ornamental gardens and orchards. The land covers 64 acres and only 16 acres of this let to Goole Urban District Council. Potter Grange sells for £5275 to Mr A W Drury.

In 1926/7, the Bennett Steamship Company extends the fleet further with the addition of the steamship the Silverthorn. The vessel built by Wood Skinner & Company Ltd. in 1908, originally bears the name 'Deux Frères'. Bretel Frères of Valognes, France owned this ship from new until 1922/3. W J Ireland then takes ownership for the next four years until he sells the vessel to Bennetts. A postcard showing the unloading of the Deux Frères can be seen in *figure 118*. The registered ship number is 147244 and the specification of the vessel can be seen in *figure 119*.

Mary Adelaide Todd (formerly Bennett) dies on the 24th August 1929, aged 60 years.

John Bentley Bennett purchases two closes of land – New Breakes Field and Stone Post Close in 1927 from the Howsin Estate[46] and in 1930, five further closes of land – Upper Sands, Middle Sands, two named Long Shores, and another Lower Thieves Dale[47] in Swinefleet.

Bennetts appear to have had a 5-year period of consolidation with the fleet remaining at these five vessels until 1932/3. At this time, Bennett's office in Hull is at 2 Nelson Street according to the local trade directory of 1928/9 (having previously been at number 11).

The balance sheet for the year ended 31st December 1930 shows more details about the company.[48] The directors of the Bennett Steamship Company are, Herbert Thomas Bennett J.P. (chairman), Georges Honoré, and John Bentley Bennett (managing director). The profit for the 12 months declared at £4,157 3s 9d.

The balance sheet also shows the fleet of steamers, Syria, Corea, Sparta, Volga and Silverthorn. They also had a lighter, Hydra, which appears to be named after one of their first vessels the Iron Screw Schooner from 1873. The value of the vessels, less depreciation is £22,500.

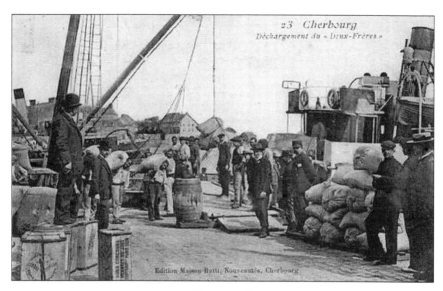

Figure 118

Figure 119

Ship No	147244
Name	Silverthorn (ex Deux Frères)
Description	Steel Screw
	Ss Hav No.3
	Ss Liv No.2
Master	
Tonnage	Gross 436, Under deck 309, net 168
Dimensions	Length – 150.0
	Breadth – 25.1
	Depth – 11.2
Engines	T3Cy14", 23 & 1/8th" & 39"-27"
	180lb 97RHP
	1SB, 3cf, GS50, HS1675
	N E Marine Engineering Co Ltd, Newcastle
Builder	Wood Skinner & Co Ltd, Newcastle
Built	1908
Owner	Bennett Steam Ship Co Ltd
Registered port	Goole
Port of survey	Hull
Class	100 A1 (built under special survey)

Their leasehold properties which comprise "Wharf, Iron Warehouse, Steam and Electric Cranes, Railway Wagons and Leasehold Office, Office Furniture, Fittings, and Plant at Goole, Boulogne s/Mer, London, and Hull" have a value of £14,562 10s 0d. There is no mention of a Paris office any longer.

In the 1930/1 Lloyds Register, the Channel Steam Ship Company Limited still appears with their one and only vessel the Whitgift. The following year, however, it has disappeared from the register. Perhaps this is not proving to be a profitable enterprise.

In recent times in connection with the area around the river Humber, 1983 sees the opening of the Humber Bridge. At that time, it was the longest single span suspension bridge in the world. What many people will not realise is that plans to build this bridge extend far back into the time of this story, and certainly involved and affected the Bennett Steamship Company, and other shipowners of the time. Around 1930, an Act comes before government which aims to provide for the construction and maintenance of a Bridge across the River Humber. It was to be a bridge without any opening with a span of 900 feet across the river at a site west of the port of Hull. Even with the relevant approach roads this would be a bridge of modest proportions compared to that of today. A petition against this Act goes before the House of Lords session of 1930-1931.[49] The petitioners are the Goole Shipowners' Association and the Goole Chamber of Commerce and Shipping. The total aggregate number of vessels of these shipowners amounts to 61, with gross registered tonnage of 52,809. The petitioners feel that this Bill will seriously affect their interests and will prejudicially interfere with their facilities.

This petition shows details of the tonnage going through the port of Goole. It states that, in 1913, the net registered tonnage of seagoing vessels paying dock dues at this port is

1,448,555 tons. Despite the economic depression brought about by the War, in 1930, there are 6,712 arrivals and departures of seagoing ships from the port. Their aggregate net registered tonnage is 2,640,708, and they carry a total cargo of 3,026,700 tons. Also at this time, the owners of the port of Goole, the Aire and Calder Navigation Company are in the process of constructing a new entrance lock which will allow vessels of 4,000 tons cargo capacity to enter.

One of the main concerns raised about the proposed bridge is that the piers and the work undertaken during construction will inevitably cause the formation of new sandbanks and alterations in the channels of the river. There is also a fear that the main channel under the bridge could develop a reduction in depth of water, or more seriously become un-navigable. Another obvious concern is that navigation under the Bridge in winter may be impossible during fog or hazy weather, and ice will not be able to flow seaward. The real fear is that Goole becomes a 'derelict port'. Representatives of both parties duly sign the petition. John Bentley Bennett is acting chairman of the aforementioned Goole Steamship Owners' Association at this time. For whatever reason, the bridge was not built until five decades later.

The Bennetts have an even bigger battle at the end of 1931 this time affecting them directly and hitting right at the heart of their own identity. It begins with the arrival of a letter on the 20th November 1931 at the offices of the Bennett Steamship Company. The letter dated 19th November comes from the War Office and reads as follows:

"Gentlemen,

I am commanded by the Army Council to inform you that it has been brought to their attention that the "Red Cross" emblem is being used by you in connection with your trade, viz., on the flags and funnels of your steamships, and to point out to you that such use of the emblem constitutes an infringement of the Geneva Convention Act, 1911.

I am, therefore, to request you to cause the "Red Cross" emblem to be eliminated wherever used in the above connection at your very earliest opportunity, and, provided that this is done and an assurance is given that there will be no further contravention of the Act, the Council are prepared to forgo further action.

I am,
Gentlemen,
Your obedient Servant
(SGD)"

The letter must have seemed like a red rag to a bull, or a naked flame to a fuse on a stick of dynamite! John Bentley Bennett, chief and managing director replies to the War Office the same day. He informs them that this insignia, adopted by his late father in 1873, has been the company's valuable and well-known trade mark for the last 58 years. He requests the Army Council to reconsider. They reply with a negative response on December 7th. John Bentley Bennett not wishing to go down without a fight states his case to the Chamber of Shipping of the United Kingdom. He noted that proceedings could not be taken except with the permission of the Attorney General. John Bentley Bennett also sends instructions to the Boulogne offices as to necessary action if required. He writes:

"It had crossed my mind to have the existing white portion of the funnel light blue, but I think this would look gaudy." He went on – *"I expect if and when we have to make the change when it is first seen on the Thames there will be rumours amongst the water side interests that the G.S.N. Company have acquired us."*

The Bennetts know of other ships also using the emblem, and Captain Wilmott of their vessel Sparta recalls passing such a ship of Scandinavian origin only a few weeks before. The

Chamber of Shipping cites other companies from Italy, Sweden, Belgium, Holland, the United States, Spain and France who are also using this emblem. The War Office again confirms their decision to the Bennett Steamship Company on the 26th January 1932. The Chamber of Shipping advises the Bennetts that they have done all they reasonably can in a letter on the 3rd February. John Bennett does not give up and proposes alternative colour schemes. The War Office writes again on 17th March 1932. John Bennett's patience is now running out. He writes to the Chamber of Shipping advising that he will not be discriminated against and will take the matter to both houses of Parliament. John Bennett writes to the War Office on 22nd March requesting an interview, as follows:

"I have information that would tend to show that my company is being discriminated against or alternatively that there is great laxity of administration."

He even threatens to close his line. He concludes *"Having regard to the fact that my company adopted the device in 1873, that the Geneva Convention was passed in the year 1911, and the matter was never raised during the European War 1914-1918 and that we are now in the year 1932, I trust the matter will not be considered one of urgency."*

The War Office advises that they are considering his representations on April 21st. On 27th June 1932, they convey their final decision. Bennetts will have to comply, and they grant them *"a reasonable period of time in which to make the necessary alterations."*

John Bennett calls upon the services of his MP Captain T.E. Sotheron-Estcourt J.P. The family associations go back to his father's generation. John Bennett and Captain Sotheron-Estcourt arrange to meet on a date which clashes with a shooting arrangement. Bennett offers to cancel it, writing on the 27th August, 1932, *"From all I hear it is going to be an exceedingly bad year for birds.*" This letter also tells of the economic situation of the company.

"*I am sorry to say Goole continues to experience the full blast of trade depression and I am laying up another steamer early in September. However it is a long lane that has no turning.*"

They already have one steamer laid up in Goole Docks. Two lain up for the 1932-33 winter, are the Corea and the Syria, the Sparta continuing the Goole-Boulogne service, leaving Goole every Saturday and Boulogne every Wednesday. The laying up of the second vessel in September indicates the termination of the 1932 fruit season, fruit forming much of the cargo at this time for the Bennett ships during the summer months.

In another letter to Sotheron-Estcourt, John Bennett tells a little more about the operations of the Bennett Company.

"*I have reduced our French-Humber services to one sailing a week for the winter months and the French-Thames services to two sailings to Boulogne and one each to Treport and Dunkirk, and with several economies effected [sic] and the help of reserves accumulated and not distributed in years gone by, if left alone, hope to continue trading in the national interest and for the benefit of the old and loyal staff we have built up over so many years; but so far as I am affected personally I have little hope of reaping any benefit.*"

By December, he arranges for the General Steam Navigation Company Ltd. to take over the London-North France services. In Lloyds Register 1933/4, listings show the Bennett fleet reduced from five to three vessels, leaving them with the Corea, Sparta and Syria. In the same register, the Silverthorn and the Volga now appear under the ownership of the General Steam Navigation Company Limited of London.

The War Office advises John Bennett, by letter dated 27th April 1933, that he has two years to change the Bennett flag. Two years later on the 27th April 1935, changes have yet to be made. John Bennett advises the War Office on the 14th May that he will make these changes within a period of seven days. The colours are to become 'mast' colour as the background on the funnels, and on the flag, a blue background with a white border. He has a small victory in that he keeps his red cross!

John Bennett writes to Georges Honoré at the Boulogne office, *"I do not know whether the present houseflag is used for any purpose at Boulogne but if so it will be well to discontinue to do so until I get the new flags. I shall order half-a-dozen. Will you let me know if you require same for Boulogne and whether you wish for more than one, they cost only 12/6 each."*

Georges Honoré replies on the 18th May 1935, *"With respect to the houseflags, we use them at Boulogne on fête-days, and it just happens that we are to put same up tomorrow for the fête of 'Jeanne d'Arc'. After that date, we shall not put them up until July 14th."*[50]

The new flag is despatched to Boulogne on May 24th 1935, on the Corea.

Around 1934/5, Bennetts give up another of their fleet, when they sell the Syria to Amos Becucci of Florence, Italy. The ship required boiler renewals and extensive refitting after having been laid up for a time. In the register, Amos has just this one vessel, registered to the port of Leghorn with an Italian flag. Perhaps he is just starting out in the shipping business. In the following year, he renames the steamer the Don Bosco.

As seen in a local trade directory of 1936, Bennetts relocate their Hull office again this time to 3 Nelson Street. They share this address with Humber Tugs Ltd. and the United Manufacturers & Distribution Association.

On the 15th May 1937, the late John and Mary Ann Bennett's son Arthur Frederick dies. His career had evolved through working for several prominent engineering companies. In 1917, he joined the Membership of the Institution of Civil Engineers.

John Bennett's four-and-a-half-year battle with the War Office is over. The company will face an even bigger battle only four years later with the onset of the Second World War. They again consolidate their business with their remaining two vessels for the years left up to the start of the War. 1937 sees the breaking up of the Volga, at Bowness.

Chapter 9
Return to Troubled Times

On the 3rd September 1939, Neville Chamberlain declares the beginning of the Second World War in a radio broadcast.

At this time, the Bennett Steamship Company owns the steamers Corea, Sparta and the lighter Hydra, the latter operating in Goole docks. The Syria, as seen earlier, has now been sold.

A mutual insurance company is undertaking measures to reduce the financial risk to ship owners at this time of war as can be seen in the Goole Times, Friday 15th September 1939.

YORKSHIRE SHIPOWNERS' MUTUAL PROTECTION SOCIETY

"The annual meeting of this Association was held at the office Customs House Buildings Monday evening last. The year's working was reviewed and satisfaction expressed at the results. The accounts were audited and arrangements made for registering the Association under the Companies' Act. Mr. Israel Jackson the secretary submitted the articles of association, which was approved by a unanimous vote. The Association is to be registered in London in the shortest possible time."

It is in the same newspaper that there also appears the following attempt to boost morale within the merchant navy.

THE KING AND THE MERCHANT NAVY
MESSAGE OF CONFIDENCE

"The following message from the King for the British Merchant Navy and the British fishing fleets was received on Monday by the president of the Board of Trade:-

In these anxious days I would like to express to all officers and men in the British Merchant Navy and the British fishing fleets my confidence in their unflinching determination to play their vital part in defence. To each one I would say: Yours is a task no less essential to my people's existence than that allotted to the Navy, Army, and Air Force. Upon you the nation depends for much of its foodstuffs and raw materials and for the transport of its troops overseas. You have a long and glorious history, and I am proud to bear the title "Master of the Merchant Navy and Fishing Fleets". I know that you will carry out your duties with resolution and fortitude, and that the high chivalrous traditions of your calling are safe in your hands.

God keep you and prosper you in your great task.

GEORGE R.I"

A Mr. Stanley has replied:

"The President of the Board of Trade, with his humble duty, has the honour to inform your Majesty that he is transmitting your Majesty's gracious and inspiring message to the officers and men of the British Merchant Navy and the British fishing fleets, and humbly begs on their behalf to express their grateful appreciation and their determination to prove worthy of your Majesty's confidence. Whatever difficulties and dangers may beset their calling, they are firmly resolved to play their part in maintaining the operations of the merchant Navy and fishing fleets, and thus to make their contribution to the achievement of victory. They will be strengthened in this resolve by the inspiration of your Majesty's message and by the renewed assurance which it gives of your Majesty's unfailing interest in all that concerns the Merchant Navy and fishing fleets."

It is likely that this message reaches all of the Bennett family and those employed by the company.

The period up to April 1940, known as the 'phoney war', sees massive air raid warnings, trenches in public parks, barrage balloons in the sky and anti-aircraft weaponry deployed on public buildings. Thirty eight million gas masks distributed to men, women, and children. Rationing of food, clothing, petrol, and other commodities suddenly becomes commonplace. Only a few months from the declaration, the war becomes acutely real for the Bennett Steamship Company. One of their vessels, the Corea, flagship of the company and loved by the staff over in Boulogne, falls victim to the hostilities. This would have affected the company and the town of Goole deeply. The Goole Times, Friday 15th December 1939 reports:

LOSS OF THE GOOLE STEAMER COREA
EIGHT LOCAL VICTIMS OF MINE

"Goole's second major disaster of the war at sea occurred early on Saturday morning when the s.s. Corea sank after striking a German mine and eight of her crew of fifteen were lost. The previous mishap was the mining of the s.s. Lowland, in which nine men were lost. All the survivors from the Corea, who were rescued by an East Coast lifeboat, reached Goole on Saturday night, with the exception of one, a Thorne man, who is detained with injuries in hospital. Some of the experiences of the survivors are described below.

News of the tragedy reached Goole during the morning and representatives of the owners, the Bennett Steamship Co. Ltd. of Goole, had the dreaded task of going round to break the sad news to the bereaved families. As was the case with the loss of the Lowland, most of the missing men were married and had

189

children. The list of the missing and the saved is as follows:

MISSING

Harry Neadham (33), captain, 18 Westfield Avenue, Goole.
Henry Watmough (26), first officer, 11 Gordon Street, Goole.
James Hosking (58), able seaman, 9 Chapel Street, Goole.
Hugh Miller (58), chief engineer, 27 Westfield Avenue, Goole.
Charles Wilson (58), acting second engineer, 58 Parliament Street, Goole.
Arthur Harrison (32), fireman, 58 Parliament Street, Goole.
John William Tomlinson (62), fireman, 23 Argyle Street, Goole.
R. Thornton, fireman, 123 Hailgate, Howden.

SAVED

Eric Heworth (30), second officer, 49 Marshfield Road, Goole.
Amos Gates, steward, 32 Jefferson Street, Goole.
T. Woodhead, able seaman, 38 Gordon Street, Goole.
E. Pantry, able seaman, 10 Estcourt Street, Goole.
S. Wimsey, able seaman, 32 Byron Street, Goole.
A. Dawson, able seaman, 92 Edinburgh Street, Goole.
J. Boxall, fireman, 25 Lower Kenyon Street, Thorne (injured and in hospital).

The Corea was Capt. Needham's first command. Aged 33, married, with two children, he had been at sea since leaving Goole Grammar School. He served in vessels of the Goole Steam Shipping, and also had two years deep sea. On returning to Goole he had a spell in the Lowland, which was sunk a fortnight ago, as chief officer. Later he joined the Bennett Steamship Co. Ltd., and served under Capt. Willmott as chief officer. When Capt. Willmott retired about four or five years ago he was given command of the Corea.

The first officer, Mr. Henry Watmough, of 11 Gordon Street, Goole, was a single man and would have been 27 years old next January. On leaving Goole Grammar School he was apprenticed in the Weir Line, and only last September he obtained his master's certificate. He had been in the Corea only a few weeks.

Mr. Hugh Miller, the chief engineer, who was 58 years of age, had been with the company for many years, and was torpedoed in the last war. He was a married man.

It is feared that a Goole man and his daughter's husband have been lost in the disaster. Mr. Charles Wilson, who was 58 years old, and lived at 58, Parliament Street, Goole, was acting second engineer on the Corea, and his son-in-law, Mr. A. Harrison who lived at the same address, was acting donkeyman. He was 32 years old. Mr. Wilson, who was married, with three children, all of whom are married, had been at sea all his working life, and had sailed with the Bennett Line nearly all that time. He was a member of the crew of the Bennett steamer Mopsa when she was mined during the last war.

Mr. Harrison, who married Mr. Wilson's daughter, had been at sea eleven years, sailing with the L.M.S. and Bennett Line steamers. He had been with the Corea since the outbreak of war. He leaves a widow and a daughter.

James Hosking, able seaman, one of the missing men, of 9, Chapel Street, Goole, is 58 years of age, and a married man with two married daughters. He had another daughter, also married, who died recently. Mr. Hosking joined the Corea on October 3rd of this year, after having been out of work for some time. He was a member of the crew of the Corea during the Great War.

John William Tomlinson, fireman on the vessel, who is also missing, lives at 23, Argyle Street and is 62 years old. He is a widower, with six grown-up children, one son being married. He has been in the employ of the Bennett Steamship Company for more than sixteen years.

Ship's fireman R. Thornton, another of the missing men, lives at 123, Hailgate, Howden. He is married, and has two children. He has lived at Howden for about two years, and formerly lived at Hemingborough. He worked for some time at the Olympia Mills, Selby, and for some months was a bus conductor in the employ of the East Yorkshire Motor Services, of Hull. He is a member of the Howden branch of the British Legion, and was formerly in the Royal Artillery. He had been at sea about six years. Mr. Thornton left Howden on November 29th to join the Corea, and his wife and children left the same day to stay with his parents at Withernsea.

SURVIVORS' STORIES
STEWARD WHO "STUCK TO THE SHIP"

In an interview shortly after being landed, Mr. Heworth said: -"I was on watch when the ship heeled over after being struck. She lurched, and three of us, Wimsey, Hosking, and I, were thrown into the water. When I came up I found a raft alongside me and I managed to climb on to it."

-"I saw the lifeboat pass and blew an S O S on my whistle, but the lifeboat crew, probably because of their engine, did not hear me. I kept on blowing as the raft drifted away, and after the lifeboat had rescued the other six survivors the crew heard my S O S and I was rescued."

-"All three of the ship's lifeboats were lifted into the air by the explosion and came down on to the water bottom up, and some of the crew clung to them."

Mr. Amos Gates, the steward, a man of 62 years of age, was one of the survivors of the Burma when she was sunk in June, 1916. On both occasions he owed his life to the fact that he remained on board the vessel and waited to be taken off.

In an interview with a "Goole Times" reporter this week, Mr. Gates, who has sailed in the company's ships for 30 years, told how five of them escaped because one of them had a torch and was able to signal to a lifeboat which had already partly turned back without seeing them.

"I had been suffering from a bad cold and I was lying in bed," said Mr. Gates, "when the explosion occurred. I jumped straight out and made a dive for my belt, but the strap had been broken away by the explosion and I had to grope for it in the dark."

"As I ran up the cabin steps the door, which had broken off, struck me on the shoulder. On deck I found two men trying to climb up on the back of the bridge. I decided in my own mind to stick to the ship, as there was no sign of any other vessels being near, although four men had already gone overboard, expecting the ship to go down straight away. The skipper was in the water and he hailed us and wanted us to join him, shouting. "We are all right here. Jump." Four men had jumped with him and we learned later that two of them died through the cold."

"Pantry, who had been with us only a couple of trips, and Woodhead, who had cut his head through being thrown up against the top of the forecastle by the explosion, were with me, and Boxall, who was injured and Dawson were also left on board."

NO SELFISHNESS

"I don't think there was a sign of selfishness among us as we stuck there in the cold, for we were only half dressed, until we saw a glimmer of light coming from another ship."

"By this time Dawson, the cook, had joined us, and luckily he had a torch with him and was able to signal to the lifeboat. It was lucky, for without that torch they would never have seen us as they had partly turned back."

"The coxswain ran his lifeboat on to the ship's side and took one of us off at a time, as there was a heavy sea and the ship had heeled over very badly. I should say it was about an hour from the time of the explosion to the time we were taken off and we were all suffering from exposure."

Mr. Gates pays a high tribute to the old coxswain of the lifeboat which took them off. "Hitler can never win the war while there are men like him about. He is a real old sea dog," he said. Mr Gates also commented on the way in which they were treated by people in the East Coast town where they were landed, and said they could not do too much for them.

Mr. Gates said that at first he thought they had been torpedoed, but now he was certain they struck a mine. He pointed out the great difficulty they all experienced because of the darkness.

Mr. James Arthur Dawson, who is 33 years of age, and was cook on the Corea, lives at, 92, Edinburgh Street, Goole. He is a married man with two children, and the Corea was sunk on his little boy's second birthday.

HELPED INJURED FIREMAN

Unassumingly, he related to a "Goole Times" representative on Tuesday how he helped the injured fireman Boxall to a place of safety, and by flashing an ordinary torch as a signal, attracted attention to his own and his mates' plight. "I had the torch to thank," he said. "I was in the forecastle when the explosion occurred. I heard the fireman moaning, saw he was injured, and helped him as best I could, pulling him to the mast. I found him a rope to hold on to. He had an ordinary torch, which I took from him, and though it had been affected by water it would still give a flash."

Dawson decided that he would have to get himself and the fireman to a higher spot, so they climbed to the starboard wing of the bridge, where they found Gates, Woodhead, and

194

Pantry. He continued to flash the torch and eventually saw the lifeboat approaching. "It came round to the starboard side," he said, "and then the torch failed."

They got on board the lifeboat, and cruised round some time looking for survivors. They found Wimsey hanging on to a bottomless box, and he was in a very bad state. A rope was thrown to him, but he had only the strength to tie it round his wrist, and he was hauled aboard the lifeboat.

"Then the coxswain of the lifeboat said he could hear a ship's whistle blowing," said Mr. Dawson. "We found Heworth (the second officer) on a raft. It was he who was blowing the whistle." Heworth was picked up and the search for survivors continued, but no one else was found. The wind and seas were terrific at the time.

CAPTAIN'S COURAGE

Mr. Dawson pays high tribute to those who assisted the men at the East Coast port where they were landed. "The head of the Shipwrecked Mariners' Society there was the best friend we had," he says. Mr. Dawson also tells how the men on the bridge had been shouting to Captain Needham, who was in the water, and how he answered back, but after the lifeboat came up they did not hear his voice any more and could not find him. Mr. Dawson has been with the Bennett Company for ten years.

Mr. Wimsey's story of the tragedy makes vivid reading. "I was just going to relieve the wheel when there was a terrific explosion. The wheelhouse was shattered to pieces and one side of the bridge was blown away. There were four of us in the wheelhouse – the skipper, the second mate, Jim Hosking, and myself. The skipper said, "Get your lifebelts on, lad, and we'll jump for it." There were three lifebelts in the wheelhouse, and we put these on while the skipper got one out of a box. Jim Hosking went overboard first. I went next with the second mate, and then the skipper came to us. The skipper was on one side of an overturned lifeboat and I was on the other side."

"Eventually I managed to grab a box, and I tried to get near the skipper with it, but I couldn't. He was shouting to the lads aboard to take a chance, and he kept up our spirits for over half an hour. I shall never understand how he went, for I was talking to him for half an hour. I was in the water an hour and I felt all right physically, although I was a bit light-headed. Then the lifeboat came and picked me up."

Mr. Wimsey was 33 years old only five days before the tragedy. An able seaman he has sailed with the Bennett steamers for fourteen months.

THORNE MAN IN HOSPITAL

Mr. John Boxall (53), of Lower Kenyon Street, Thorne, a survivor, has cheated death in the sea for the second time in two wars. Mr. Boxall, who is a ship's fireman, is in hospital suffering from injuries and shock. His wife has received a message from the matron of the hospital that he is comfortable and progressing satisfactorily. Mr. Boxall should have arrived home on Wednesday, and his wife was definitely expecting him on Saturday, thinking that the rough weather had delayed the ship's homecoming, but instead she was visited by a representative of the owners of the Corea, who told her what had happened.

When seen by a reporter Mrs. Boxall stated that her husband was not afraid of the submarine menace, and the last time he was at home said that he would never be drowned at sea.

Mrs. Boxall said that on the outbreak of the war in 1914 her husband came off what she believed to be the sister ship of the Corea the day before it went to sea and was sunk.

WELL-KNOWN GOOLE SHIP

The Corea was on a voyage with general cargo from Boulogne to Goole when she was mined.

The Corea had for many years traded out of Goole under the Bennett Line flag. She was a fine, speedy vessel and was used almost solely on the Goole-Boulogne trade. During the last war she rendered excellent and her gross tonnage 751. She was built in 1895 by Earle's Shipbuilding and Engineering Co., Ltd., of Hull.

The Bennett Line lost four steamers during the last war, three of them by enemy action and one by a collision while steaming without lights. Those mined or torpedoed were the Mopsa, Africa, and Burma, and that sunk in collision was the Malta. No loss of life attended the sinking of the Mopsa or Malta, but about eight lives were lost when the other two vessels went down.

Previous local sea tragedies of the war affecting Goole included the loss of the Lowland with nine lives. She was mined off the East Coast in the same manner as was the Corea. Two Goole men lost their lives when, early in the war, the motor vessel Brendonia was sunk after a collision in the blackout by an unknown steamer.

TOWN'S SYMPATHY

At a meeting of Goole Town Council on Wednesday evening the Mayor referred to the two recent sea disasters Goole had sustained, and said Goole seamen during the past few months had been facing unheard of dangers. "We as a town are proud of our fellow townsmen for their work in bringing foodstuffs and risking their lives. Only by the loss of the steamers Lowland and Corea – two local vessels manned by Goole men – do we realise the dangers of their calling. We sympathise with the families of those men who have lost their lives in these two disasters." The Council stood for a moment in silent tribute."

197

From information kindly supplied by his daughter-in-law, Captain Needham was the youngest captain to sail out of Goole and the Corea the first ship to pass through Ocean Lock at Goole. She also has the last letter sent from France by Captain Needham to his family just to say 'we are still on top' (this taken to mean that they had so far survived sinking). The letter arrives with his family after the fateful sinking of the vessel.

The Bennett Steamship Company release their year end results three weeks later on 31st December 1939.[51] These give quite a lot of information about the company at this time. The revenue account stands at only £96:4:11 at the end of 1938, and for 1939 £1,629:18:2 added. This makes total net revenue only £2,029:18:2, less than half the amount nine years earlier, and the war just beginning. To go into a period of war in such a fragile state must have been a tremendous worry to the Board of Directors. The value of assets drops dramatically too. Only three vessels appear in the list for 1939, the Corea, Sparta and Hydra, however, a line below details the Corea 'lost by enemy action' as seen from the account previously mentioned. The other assets of wagons, plant, and offices have also dropped from nine years earlier to £9,351:10:9. There is no longer a London office listed. The company is virtually on its knees. The directors at this time, Herbert Thomas Bennett, John Bentley Bennett, and Georges Louis Honoré, must have had grave concerns for the viability of the company.

Key employees of the company in 1940 can be seen from the Company papers. Georges Louise Honoré of 53 Boulevard Daunon, Boulogne, is Steamship Manager over in France. As seen previously, one of the directors of the company, Charles Thomas Everist, of 4 Lloyds Avenue, London, is Steamship Manager in London although a London office no longer appears. Long serving employee Albert Gunnill of 9 Cholemley Street, Hull, is Steamship Manager in the Hull office. Present at John Bennett's funeral in 1904 and listed as 'staff' shows that he is with the company for at least 36 years.

During heavy bombardment in May 1940, all the installations, offices and sheds of the Basin Loubet France disappear in flames. This must have been a crippling blow to the company.

In the following month, the Sparta takes part in 'Operation Ariel'. She makes one voyage from Brest to Falmouth with evacuated troops on 17th-18th June 1940.

The balance sheet for 31st December 1940 shows that the situation has deteriorated even further. Having written off the value of the Corea, £7000, this leaves the remaining two vessels with a combined value of £8,825:0:0. The plant and offices have maintained their value of the previous year (the usual depreciation perhaps not applied to make the company look a bit healthier than it would otherwise). The net revenue now stands at only £604:1:8.

The loss of one of the two remaining vessels, the Sparta, occurs less than three months later. The Goole Times, Friday 14th March 1941 reports the account:

BELIEVED VICTIMS OF WAR AT SEA

"A further list of Goole men who are reported missing as the result of enemy action at sea is as follows:-

Mr. Frank Haigh, a chief officer, of 50 Westbourne Grove, Goole.
Mr. W.J. Needham, a chief engineer, of 130 Dunhill Road, Goole.
Mr. H.J. Knott, a donkeyman, of 14 Phoenix Street, Goole.
Mr. Amos Gates, a steward, of 32 Jefferson Street, Goole.

Mr. Frank Haigh was 28 years of age and an old boy of Goole Grammar School. He served his apprenticeship with a Cardiff firm and soon after obtaining his ticket he joined his last company. He had been with them for six years. A married man, he leaves a wife and a two-and-a-half-year-old daughter.

Mr. William John Needham was 60 years of age and a chief engineer. A wife and one son are left. Mr. Needham had been going to sea since 1899 and had sailed with numerous local vessels. He was a member of the Aire and Calder Lodge of Freemasons.

Mr. Herbert John Knott, aged 52, had been with the company, with the exception of a short break, for over twenty years. He was at sea during the last war and was mined when sailing in the French Rose. This is the second tragedy his wife had witnessed recently, for less than a month ago her youngest son, Tom, was also lost at sea.

Mr. Amos Gates, aged 62, was for over thirty years in the service of the Bennett Steamship Co., Ltd. He was one of the survivors of the s.s. Burma when she was sunk in 1916, and again in December, 1939 he was one of the seven saved when the s.s. Corea was mined. On that occasion he owed his life to the fact that one of five of them had a torch and was able to signal for help to a lifeboat which had gone to the rescue of the sinking vessel, and he paid high tribute to the pluck and skill of the coxswain of the lifeboat which took them off."

Mr Amos Gates had given a lifetime of service to the company. He survived the sinking of the Burma, also the mining of the Corea. Unfortunately, this was not the case with the third incident. His grand daughter kindly supplied photographs of her grandfather Amos *figures 120 & 121.*

On its final journey, the Sparta was steaming from Blyth to Southampton with a cargo of coal.

Figure 120   Figure 121

The real damage to the company as a result of the effects of
the war can be seen in the balance sheet of 31st December
1941. The value of the Sparta, £8,825, written off the assets
leaves only one vessel the Lighter Hydra valued at £8,825.
During this year, the company receives a final instalment of
War Risk Insurance on the Sparta of £3,702:13:2. This
suggests that the Sparta was under the orders of the War
Office when lost. The company did not receive a payment of
this kind for the Corea at the time of her loss. Also on this
account is a sum of £1700 credited by the Government for
'tonnage replacement'. This is another indication that work
they carry out is for the war effort. The results for 1941 show
the net revenue of £1010:0:5, just slightly better than that of
the previous year. In 1941, the directors are John Bentley
Bennett, and George Louis Honoré.

The bombing raids of the Hull "blitz" totally destroy the
Bennett Steamship Company berth at Riverside Quay. This

must have occurred during 1942 as the balance sheet at the end of this year shows only offices and plant at Goole and Boulogne. No vessels appear. The net revenue account has now fallen to an unbelievable £203:11:4. The covering summary states "The Company continue to operate certain vessels on behalf of The Minister of War Transport but otherwise its activities are restricted by existing war conditions". This is probably disguising the dreadful reality of the situation.

The Hydra has totally disappeared during this time, and not a single vessel appears under the Bennett Steamship Company in Lloyds Register of 1941/2. The following year, however, the steamship Léoville appears in the register owned by the Ministry of War Transport but managed by Bennetts. Previously owned by Worms & Company of Le Havre, it appears that the War Ministry requisitioned the vessel for the war effort. The specification of this vessel can be seen in the table *figure 122*.

Figure 122

Ship No	168088
Name	ss Léoville
Tonnage	Gross 1050, Under deck 796, net 417
Dimensions	Length – 216.0 Breadth – 30.8 Depth – 12.6
Engines	T.3Cy.18", 30" & 50"-33" 144 NHP by Atel & Ch. De la Seine Maritime
Builder	Atel & Ch. De la Seine Maritime Le Trait S/I
Built	1922
Owner	Ministry of War Transport (Bennett Steam Ship Co Ltd Mgrs)
Registered port	Glasgow

The balance sheet of 31st December 1943 also shows the Government 'Tonnage Replacement' payment of £1700. No vessels appear. The plant and offices listed is the same as the previous year. Net revenue has gone up slightly from the previous year to £806:6:4.

In this year, another vessel appears in the register owned by the Ministry of War Transport but under the management of the Bennett Steamship Company. This vessel, the steamship Pessac, was also previously owned by Worms & Company of Le Havre. The Ministry requisitioned her in 1940 at Plymouth, and the Bennett Steamship Company in London managed her in 1941. The Pessac suffers severe damage by enemy bombing in Plymouth on the evening of 29th April 1941, and subsequently sinks. Repaired she returns to service in December 1942. The ship's specification can be seen in the table *figure 123*.

Figure 123

Ship No	168327
Name	ss Pessac
Type	3 Mast
Tonnage	Gross 859, Under deck 501, net 356
Dimensions	Length – 197.8 Breadth – 28.0 Depth – 12.1
Engines	T.3Cy.15", 23.5" & 39"-27.5" 81 NHP by Forges Et Chantiers De La Méditerranée Havre
Builder	Forges Et Chantiers De La Méditerranée Havre
Built	1907
Owner	Ministry of War Transport (Bennett Steam Ship Co Ltd Mgrs)
Registered port	London

The Pessac was armed with four guns of 100mm, two guns of 37mm, four machine guns of 8mm and two mortars.

In June 1944, the town of Boulogne witnesses the utter destruction of its richest quarter. This includes the fine building of the Bennett Company offices situated on the Rue Victor Hugo. The hotel and conference chamber belonging to the Bennett Steamship Company, often used for various industrial, literary and philanthropic committees in the town, also falls victim to the bombardment. Some company account books survive, however, in a box found in the debris.

Albert Chatelle writes that Monsieur Georges Honoré sadly relates to the Chamber of Commerce "Of the Bennett Steamship Company there remains therefore literally nothing."

Not long after, on 3rd December 1944, John Bentley Bennett dies following a brief illness.

In February 1945, an incident occurs in Ostend connected with the Léoville, under the command of Master Charles Hudson. Many years later the Goole Times of 16th October 1997 relates the story told by Captain Hudson as follows:

"In a letter he sent to the Bennett Steam Ship Company Ltd., in February 1945 when he was master of the Léoville ...he describes how his vessel was discharging a cargo of high explosives when a nearby petrol and ammunition depot caught fire and "commenced to explode with great violence, showering the vessel with burning debris and splinters so that the vessel, her cargo and all personnel in the vicinity were in great danger." He then explains how he and his men managed to get their ship out of the immediate area, and states "all the crew are worthy of the highest praise. But for the prompt and courageous action of all these men, there is no doubt, the vessel would have blown up and many more lives lost." 54 individuals lose their lives "on other vessels berthed at a much greater distance away from the depot than our vessel."

From information kindly given by Captain Hudson's son, the crew put their captain forward for a medal. The captain also recommends that all of his crew receive medals for their bravery. No medals are forthcoming. Captain Hudson's son also recounts how his father told him that the Léoville was "the starboard command ship of the invasion" and that they spent eight days laid up on a beach and under fire from the enemy. His father was also in command of a vessel seized from the enemy, the steamship Adler, subsequently used as a troop carrier. The Adler, infested with rats whilst laid up at Hull, had to be taken out into the river Humber for fumigation to allow her to be put back into service.

The Second World War (in Europe) ends on 8th May 1945. By this period, the company is in tatters. A notice dated 31st May 1945 calls for an Extraordinary General Meeting of the Company. The death of John Bentley Bennett leaves the company without any director in England. There is some doubt about the status of Monsieur Georges Honoré as a director of the company due to his residency in France, a country under German occupation for some time. The company has to appoint new directors and nominate three individuals. Mr John Taylor Bennett, son of Herbert Thomas Bennett (late chairman of the Company), Mr George William Dunham, Company Secretary for 26 years, and Mr Charles Thomas Everist. Mr Everist, associated with the company for 37 years, spent 18 of those as Manager of the Company's London Office.

In order to safeguard the interests of shareholders, the inevitable decision finally comes in 1945 for the voluntary winding-up of the company. Legal representatives draw up a Declaration of Solvency at the end of August and Charles Thomas Everist, George William Dunham and John Taylor Bennett sign it. These directors declare that there are sufficient funds to pay off all the company's debts within a 12-month period. The commencement of the winding up begins on 27th September 1945. On the 4th October, William Felix

Pearce, of Atlas Chambers, King Street, Leeds, Chartered Account, and George William Dunham take on the role of liquidators to the Bennett Steamship Company Limited. The fact that George Dunham is a loyal and trusted employee, having served with the company for many years, perhaps explains his appointment to this final act.

Albert Chatelle tells of this sad decision when Monsieur Honoré writes in 1946 to the Chamber of Commerce "I regret to have to inform you that the Bennett Steamship Company, particularly by submarine warfare, will shortly cease to exist." He continues "the fleet of our old Anglo/Boulogne Society have totally disappeared in the course of two World Wars, in addition our Offices and Warehouses at Hull have been destroyed by aerial bombardment and those at Boulogne have not escaped total destruction."

From 4th October 1945 to March 28th 1946, the Liquidators realize assets to the value of £65,729:9:2. The disbursements paid out in the same period amount to £40,547:7:2. This leaves a balance of £25,182:2:0 plus an estimate in remaining assets – investments, freehold property, debts and cash at the bank, of £35,000. On the 7th November 1946, the Liquidators certify that shareholders are to be paid at a rate of £7:10:0 per share. They provide a comprehensive list of all those shareholders and the value of their shares at this time. The first part of the list details English shareholders with the late John Bennett's surviving children holding quite a number of shares:

Herbert Thomas Bennett	235	value	£1,762:10:0
Isabel Tupholme	216	value	£1,620
Edith Elizabeth Spinks	206	value	£1,545
Mary Eleanor Orsmby	169	value	£1,267:10:0

Former employees have also invested heavily in the company:

| George William Dunham | 70 | value | £525 |

Charles Thomas Everist	50	value £375
Herbert Gunhill	25	value £187:10:0
Georges Louis Honoré	275	value £2,062:10:0

Both Herbert Thomas Bennett and his sister Isabel Tupholme die in 1946.

Virtually none of the French shareholders claim their share value during the first 6-month period. These account lists continue at 6-monthly intervals showing further realization of assets, disbursements and the shareholders having made a claim. The assets realized were in the main, investments and Defence Bonds. Disbursements continue to be paid and in the period Sept 1946 to March 1947, the 'Custodian of Enemy Property' paid £2,095:18:10 for sundry creditors in France at the date of liquidation. This same recipient also receives £199:14:0 for unpaid dividends that are due to French shareholders (some of this subsequently repaid due to an error in the claim). George Louis Honoré also receives a payment on 5th March for 'Compensation Boulogne Staff' totalling £395:16:7. In the six months up to September 1947, the majority of French shareholders claim their shares. From the 17th February 1947, shares depreciate to £2:10:0 probably due to the diminishing value of remaining assets. The 27th September 1950, sees the sale of 3, Nelson Street, Hull to the Hull Corporation for £2,817:2:6, so despite the Hull bombings and the earlier report that the Hull offices and dock installations destroyed, some Hull offices it would seem were not entirely lost. The Liquidators had to pay out of the proceeds of the sale, surveyors costs of £77:14:0 to John Watson & Carter, and legal charges (relating to the sale) of £75 to Maw, Redman & Morfitt. The Liquidators declare a final distribution of £1:11:4 per share in October 1950. British shareholders are the first to receive settlement, with the payment of final distribution to shareholders resident abroad made during the period Sept 1951 to March 1952.

The final company account shows that they realised a value of £77,806:11:5 from 27th September 1945 to 6th December 1952. All creditors paid, and with charges relating to the winding-up, and the distribution of shares at £1:11:4 per £10 share to shareholders, this totalled £69,400. The final General Meeting of the Company, called for 8th January 1953, declares the completion of the liquidation.

Escombe Lambert fills the gap in the shipping operations and by the Christmas following the remaining Bennett staff disbanded. The Bennett Steamship Company had finally taken its last breath. After building up to a prosperous and successful shipping company from its birth as the Red Cross Line, it slowly began to crumble as the toll of two world wars took effect. One by one the workhorses of the company – the steamships – began to disappear, either as a result of enemy action or through selling off. John Bennett's dream now lies at the bottom of the sea – asleep in the deep.

Eternal Father, strong to save,
Whose arm hath bound the restless wave,
Who bidd'st the mighty ocean deep
Its own appointed limits keep;
Oh, hear us when we cry to Thee,
For those in peril on the sea!

From the hymn ~
"Eternal Father, Strong to Save" by William Whiting 1860

Figure 124

ILLUSTRATION SOURCES & ACKNOWLEDGEMENTS

REFERENCE NOTES

1   OA–247–112 by kind permission of West Yorkshire Archive Service, Wakefield.
2   C236/3/1 by kind permission of West Yorkshire Archive Service, Wakefield.
3   UL 640/769 by kind permission of West Yorkshire Archive Service, Wakefield.
4   XE 447/469 by kind permission of West Yorkshire Archive Service, Wakefield.
5   DDX1298/2/3/4 by kind permission of ERALS.
6   DDCL/1026 by kind permission of ERALS.
7   Albert Chatelle – 'La Compagnie Bennett et le port de Boulogne 1947'. English translation by Printers 'Acheve d'imprimer sur les presses de l'Imprimerie du littoral a Boulogne-sur-Mer' source Goole Waterways Museum.
8   666/643/731 by kind permission of West Yorkshire Archive Service, Wakefield.
9   666/642/730 by kind permission of West Yorkshire Archive Service, Wakefield.
10   711/250/294 by kind permission of West Yorkshire Archive Service, Wakefield.
11   715/405/445 by kind permission of West Yorkshire Archive Service, Wakefield.
12   DDX1298/2/5/1 by kind permission of ERALS.
13   GRO 1871 Qtr 1 Doncaster vol 9C page 575.
14   GRO 1873 Qtr 3 Fylde vol 8E page 627.
15   GRO 1874 Qtr 1 Goole vol 9C page 738.
16   GRO 1875 Qtr 3 Ormskirk vol 8B page 729.
17   742/4/7 by kind permission of West Yorkshire Archive Service, Wakefield.
18   751/130/138 by kind permission of West Yorkshire Archive Service, Wakefield.
19   758/538/662 by kind permission of West Yorkshire Archive Service, Wakefield.
20   DDX1298/2/3/6 by kind permission of ERALS.
21   773/525/618 by kind permission of West Yorkshire Archive Service, Wakefield.
22   773/517/613 by kind permission of West Yorkshire Archive Service, Wakefield.
23   795/226/261 by kind permission of West Yorkshire Archive Service, Wakefield.
24   Information from "Glimpses of Old and New Dundee" by A H Millar.
25   Plaque on Belvedere House wording by historian Malcolm

Neesam who has kindly given permission to reproduce via the Harrogate Civic Society.

26   John Bennett's will 1883 ref. DX/BAX/62396/14/35 from Doncaster Metropolitan Borough Council Archives who have kindly given permission to use.

27   C236/28/1 by kind permission of West Yorkshire Archive Service, Wakefield.

28   DDBT by kind permission of ERALS.

29   GRO 1885 Qtr 3 Southport vol 8b page 817.

30   From information supplied by the Royal Archives.

31   12/4/4 by kind permission of West Yorkshire Archive Service, Wakefield.

32   28/473/225 by kind permission of West Yorkshire Archive Service, Wakefield.

33   35/457/245 by kind permission of West Yorkshire Archive Service, Wakefield.

34   DDX1298/2/3/10 by kind permission of ERALS.

35   The Daily News 30th August 1894 by kind permission of Daily News/Associated Newspapers Ltd.

36   Crew Agreements 1895/6 ss China source National Maritime Museum, Greenwich, London. ©Crown Copyright - The National Archives.

37   DDX1298/2/5/2 by kind permission of ERALS.

38   La Voix Maritime 25th September 1975. Also published prior to this in the Boulogne Review p.297, December 1948 as part of the serialisation of Albert Chatelle's pamphlet 'La Compagnie Bennett et le port de Boulogne'.

39   Note written on the auction catalogue ref. DDX1298/2/5/4 by kind permission of ERALS.

40   DDX1298/2/5/3 by kind permission of ERALS.

41   All Shipping Notices kindly provided by Goole Waterways Museum.

42   Denmark House Grade Listing ref TQ3280SE 636-1/17/771 reproduced by kind permission of English Heritage ©Crown copyright. NMR.

43   Goole & Howden Chronicle 8th January 1987.

44   DDX1298/2/7/3 by kind permission of ERALS.

45   DDX1298/2/5/10 by kind permission of ERALS.

46   DDX1298/2/5/11 by kind permission of ERALS.

47   DDX1298/2/5/12 by kind permission of ERALS.

48   Company papers 1939-1953 ref. BT31/35952/31137 ©Crown Copyright kindly provided by The National Archives.

49   Parliamentary material - House of Lords Session 1930-31 "Humber Bridge Petition of the Goole Steamship Owners' Association and the Goole Chamber of Commerce and

Shipping" kindly provided by The National Archives, Kew.

50 Article "Bennett Line's Fight for its Flag' from Sea Breezes Oct 1968 pages 604-612. By kind permission of Steve Robinson Editorial Manager Sea Breezes Publications Ltd.

51 Company papers 1939-1953 ref. BT31/35952/31137 ©Crown Copyright kindly provided by The National Archives.

QUOTATIONS & OTHER SOURCES

Albert Chatelle – 'La Compagnie Bennett et le port de Boulogne'. English translation by Printers 'Acheve d'Imprimer sur les presses de l'Imprimerie du littoral a Boulogne-sur-Mer, le 20 Decembre 1947'. Also serialised in the Boulogne Review 1948-9.

Goole & Marshland Times, Goole Weekly Times, Goole Times, Goole Times Illustrated Almanack, The Selby Express and The Howdenshire Gazette all articles copyright of and reproduced by kind permission of Chronicle Publications Limited. This material was sourced from Goole Local Studies Library and the author acknowledges their extensive assistance.

Excerpts from the Diary of Edith Elizabeth Bennett 1892 reproduced by kind permission of her grand daughter Rosamund Jennings.

Boulogne Review – CCI Cote d'Opale, 24 Boulevard des Alliés, B.P. 199 62104 Calais Cedex.

All quotations and information from Kelly's directories with kind permission of Kelly's Industrial Directories, Reed Business Information.

With grateful thanks also to Pat Needham (daughter-in-law of Captain Needham), Mr Hudson (son of Captain Hudson), Steven Goulden (GG Grandson of Herbert Thomas Bennett) and Christine Dent (Granddaughter of Amos Gates) who all kindly contacted me in response to my newspaper advertisement and kindly gave information.

Thanks also to all the numerous family members that I have been in contact with over the last few years and who have kindly shared information with me.

The author and publisher gratefully acknowledge the permission granted to reproduce the copyright material in this book. Every effort has been made to trace copyright holders and to obtain their permission for the use of copyright material. The publisher apologises for any errors or omissions in the above list and would be grateful if notified of any corrections that should be incorporated in future reprints or editions of this book.